IF YOU FORGET EVERYTHING ELSE REMEMBER THIS

KATHARINE HILL

IF YOU FORGET EVERYTHING ELSE REMEMBER THIS

PARENTING IN THE PRIMARY YEARS

Muddy
Pearl

First published in 2015 by
Muddy Pearl, Edinburgh, Scotland.
www.muddypearl.com
books@muddypearl.com

First Edition 2015
Reprinted 2015, 2016, 2020
Second Edition 2022

British Library Cataloguing in Publication Data
A catalogue record for this book is available from the British Library
ISBN 978-1-914553-11-0

Typeset in Minion by Revo Creative Ltd, Lancaster
Printed in Great Britain by Bell & Bain Ltd, Glasgow

To Jo Jane and Ginny – fourteen children between us, and now twelve grandchildren and counting! Thanks for your friendship and support during the ups and downs of parenting in the the primary years.

ACKNOWLEDGEMENTS

This book has been a lot of fun to write – a heartfelt thank you to all those who have helped make it possible. Thank you to Rob Parsons for his help and encouragement, and for writing the foreword.

Thank you to the amazing team at Care for the Family – especially to Paula Pridham and Sheron Rice. And for this second edition many thanks to Sarah Rowlands, Samantha Callan, Vicky Lavy and my PA Jody Jones.

I am grateful to Stephanie Heald and the team at Muddy Pearl – for your care, creativity and attention to detail – it's great working with you. And to David McNeill for the wonderful cartoons that make me laugh out loud.

And as ever, thank you to Team Hill (which has increased in number since the first edition!) – Richard, George, Ellie, Eva, and Arabella, Charlotte, Will, Ezra and Tabitha Caldwell, Ed, Catriona and Finn and Henry – without you the book couldn't possibly have been written!

CONTENTS

FOREWORD

Last month our washing machine stopped working. That little event sent me trawling through the kitchen drawers looking for the instruction manual that I was sure that I had put 'somewhere safe.' When I eventually found it I discovered that somebody had torn off the pages that were in English and left me with a choice of Spanish or Mandarin.

It was frustrating, but I can tell you that there were times in our parenting that I'd have settled for an instruction manual in any language. In fact I wish that my wife, Dianne, and I had owned a copy of *Remember This* when our kids were small. In this wonderful book, Katharine tackles the big issues that affect every parent of primary age children. But this is not just another parenting book – this book oozes wisdom, practical help and above all, understanding. There are times in all our parenting when we wish that either we could have another go at it – or at least that there was somewhere we could go to discover help with the everyday challenges and blessings of being a parent. How can we give our children strong roots that will help them face the storms of life – not to mention the trauma of the teenage years? How should we deal with the testing toddler who tries us daily? What is the best way to set (and enforce!) boundaries? How can we get our children ready for the world out there so they can stand on their own two feet? How do our children come to believe that they are loved? Katharine tackles these issues and a dozen more.

This book made me laugh (the cartoons are brilliant!), and at times it moved me greatly, but I think what I love most about it is that it's so very down-to-earth. We need answers to some of the dilemmas we face as parents – and this book gives us those. But even more important is the life-changing, liberating news that we are not alone: even if we are struggling a bit at this stage of our parenting, others have worn that tee-shirt and come through it. And Katharine has worn the tee-shirt, not just as a mother of four but somebody who has spoken (and listened) to thousands of parents.

I hope you enjoy it.

Rob Parsons, OBE
Founder and Chairman, Care for the Family

INTRODUCTION

The day that changed everything was 3rd September. That day goes down in the annals of history for a number of reasons. It not only marks the demise of Oliver Cromwell, the setting of a new world land speed record, and the beginning of the Second World War, but it is also the day that I became a parent. After the elation of seeing the pregnancy test turn blue, followed by months of enduring what is commonly known as 'morning' sickness (a misnomer if ever there was one), I was looking forward with excitement to my first child's arrival. Nothing, however, prepared me for what was to follow.

The week before, I'd had a busy full-time job and (with the exception of the morning sickness) felt fully in control of my world. But at thirty-seven weeks pregnant, rock-and-rolling at a friend's wedding seemed to be all that was needed to kick-start the onset of labour, and eight hours later I found myself gazing at the little red and wrinkled bundle that was our son.

What I didn't know was the extent to which life was about to change … forever. This baby had taken longer to conceive than I had imagined, and the monthly rollercoaster of hope and anticipation followed by crashing disappointment had become an unwelcome but familiar routine. I naïvely assumed that the struggle to conceive and eight-and-a-half months of nausea followed by a night of hard labour meant that the difficult bit was over, and I looked forward to life as a mother with a mixture of excitement and anticipation. I had had antenatal advice by the bucketload on the practical challenges of the first few weeks –

feeding, bathing, changing – all mastered while enduring acute sleep deprivation which seemed to put Special Forces training in the shade.

Useful as that was, my focus on the few weeks following the birth meant that I had somehow overlooked the fact that this was just the beginning. The journey of parenthood had really only just begun. If I thought that babies and toddlers were challenging, that was only because I hadn't yet tried to get a four-year-old unstuck from a lamp post and into his first day at school, stayed up till the small hours trying to make my son a Bart Simpson mask for the school play 'like Leo's mummy can make', or realized that my ten-year-old was serious when he told me that his classmate, Charlie, knew where he could get weed – and he wasn't referring to the classroom allotment.

In the whirlwind of life as a parent, for not one or two but eventually four children (what *were* we thinking?), and amid the chaos of finding swimming goggles, making packed lunches, cleaning out the rabbit, refereeing sibling squabbles, delousing hair and mending broken laces, what I have longed for (other than a good night's sleep and some adult conversation) has been a book that I could pick up quickly and easily to find some wisdom to help me navigate this wonderful but challenging season of life. In the same way that the ancient book of Proverbs gives bite-sized principles for living, I needed something that would give me principles for parenting and family life.

I wanted a book of short and to-the-point sayings that I could read in a few minutes while waiting for the kettle to boil – sayings that I could commit to memory and draw upon at a second's notice. This is that book: a series of short chapters offering memorable sayings that will bring direction and clarity to us in our important role as parents and carers. I have tried to make each chapter heading a catchphrase that can be easily recalled in an instant amid the busyness, exhaustion and chaos that go with the territory of parenting in the primary years.

So fill the kettle, make a cup of tea, turn the page, and if you forget everything else as a parent, remember this …

FASTEN YOUR SEAT BELTS

Fasten your seatbelts

Just recently, I was sitting in my car outside a school and witnessed a wonderful scene. A man was walking towards me. Dressed for a day at the office, he looked confident, as if he had it all together. Yet it wasn't a briefcase he was holding, but the hand of a little girl, who looked about four years old.

I watched them as they left the pavement and made their way down the little path towards the school door. They walked a few paces, then he bent and whispered into her ear, and then they walked on a little further. And suddenly it dawned on me: it was her first day at school. As they reached the entrance, I don't know which of them was the most reluctant to let go, but finally she skipped into school with a wave, and a teacher took her hand and led her into the classroom. The man waved too and blew a kiss at the closed door. And then he moved to a nearby window and I saw him waving again and smiling. His chest swelled with pride as he watched her. And so all was well – a milestone reached and another child launched successfully into a new season. He turned and began walking back towards me.

And that's when I saw him brush away a tear.

I sat in the car for a moment and thought about that little scene. Of course, in many ways it wasn't special at all – it was being repeated at a thousand school gates across the country. And yet I knew I had witnessed something profound. The smile, the wave and the tear sum up the incredible task of parenting – fun times, sad times, and every step of the way, getting ready for the day when we have to let them go.

My mind went back to my son's first day at school and another thought occurred to me. This was just the start. If that father was thinking that moment marked the end of the baby years, and this was the last time he would feel such a swing of emotion, then he was wrong. The weeks, months and years ahead would be full of waves, smiles and tears, but so much more: times of unimaginable pleasure, fulfilment, laughter and deep joy, closely followed by periods of exhaustion, frustration, guilt and despair … and back again. It goes with the territory of parenthood. You will have your heart filled with joy and then broken, and then put back together, again and again. A quote popularly attributed to Elizabeth Stone puts it well: 'Making the decision to have a child – it is momentous. It is to decide forever to have your heart go walking around outside your body.'

Parenting is also a long-haul business. Sometimes at Care for the Family events, we ask parents of pre-schoolers to raise their hands. Then we ask them if they are looking forward (just a bit!) to the time when the children are grown and standing on their own two feet. Weary parents raise their hands – and sometimes I can see just the hint of a hope of a day when they won't have to worry about these little ones. When their hands are lowered we ask if there are any parents in the audience with children in their thirties or even forties. There are always some grandparents present who will obligingly raise their hands. Then we ask them, 'Do you still worry about your children?'

In all the years we have been doing this, we have never been disappointed with the answer: 'More than ever!' We then turn to the newer parents and say, 'And that's why you must pace yourself – it really is a long-haul business!'

Life as a parent is a rollercoaster – moments of incredible joy, fun and laughter followed by times of tears, worry and pain and back again. Tantrums, whining and sibling rivalry one minute; an angelic role in the nativity play the next; frantic trips to A&E and anxious minutes in the hospital waiting room; celebration at success and disappointment at failure; reassurance at milestones met, gut-wrenching worry when they are missed; loyal friendships and cliques, fallings out and school bullies; battles over screen time and worries about mental health; first loves and broken hearts; flooded campsites and holidays in the sun – and all this played out against the backdrop of living in our beautiful and yet broken world. There's nothing else like it – it's the ride of a lifetime. So hold on tight and fasten your seatbelts!

'Have a safe trip and enjoy your new life with the little one.'

HOSPITAL

REMEMBER
WHO
YOU
ARE

Remember who you are

Donna was a teenage parent who came to a recent Care for the Family parenting event. She was at least ten years younger than the rest of the women there, and, I confess, I wondered just how helpful the event would be for her. At the end of the evening she proudly showed me a picture of her little boy, sitting in the bath, covered with bath foam and grinning from ear to ear. What she said next surprised me. She commented that the most helpful part of the evening was when we spoke about how easy it is in the early days of parenthood to feel a loss of confidence and identity. She had been a student when she had her baby, and had been catapulted, almost overnight, from her course on fashion and design to the responsibility of parenthood. She said, 'I didn't realize it was happening – I didn't have time to, but somewhere along the way I lost myself. It was such a relief to hear that was normal.' This loss of confidence is not simply the preserve of young single parents like Donna, but seems to engulf mothers everywhere. Mothers, regardless of age, background or life experience, find themselves asking the same question: 'Who am I?'

Many women in particular find that when they become a parent for the first time, their confidence and self-esteem is dealt a surprising blow. We wonder if our bodies will ever return to their pre-baby shape (answer: probably not), and our ability to think clearly or engage in any rational conversation may seem to have deserted us. It can take time for our confidence to return.

The process of regaining confidence after having children can never be a quick fix. But if you find yourself feeling low or tearful for more than a few weeks, it is worth asking for help. Postnatal depression is very common and with the right support, it does get better.

Whatever our situation there are practical things we can do that can help us. Looking back, finding 'child-free' moments certainly helped me in the quest to rediscover my sense of self. As much as I wholeheartedly embraced this stage of life and loved being a parent, those moments were a welcome reminder that there was life beyond children. A weekly mums' group with a crèche was an oasis in the week, with an opportunity to make new friends and share experiences. A regular arrangement with a friend also paid dividends. I would look after her children one Wednesday afternoon and she had mine the next.

Full-blown chaos in the house one week was rewarded on the alternate week with some time to ourselves when we could shop, have a bath, read, write, tidy the house, watch TV, drink coffee or sleep, uninterrupted and unencumbered. Bliss! In my experience, this loss of identity is often the preserve of mothers, but some dads also can find the adjustment to the responsibility of parenthood, and the change in family priorities a challenge.

There is no shortage of advice as to how to regain this loss of identity and it often involves keeping your hand in at your previous job or career or reminding yourself how successful you once were. Suggestions I came across included meeting up with former work colleagues to catch up on the latest 'news', returning to my maiden name and even getting a tattoo.[1]

One friend suggested I keep a copy of my professional qualification certificate framed in the loo and look at it daily to remind myself of what I once achieved. Frankly, these suggestions failed because they fell into the trap of assuming that my identity is based on my previous life. But it's not. I am a woman with gifts, hopes and aspirations. My identity isn't in my paid job, as much as I enjoy it, and it is not in my children either. And if it was in either of those things, then the day I lost that job or my children left home I would lose … me. No, I decided to put a different poster on the loo wall: 'Katharine, you were enough before you had your job and before you had your kids – there is nothing to prove.' (OK, I didn't actually hang it up – but there were times I wish I had!)

Over the years, I have been a full-time parent, and I have worked outside the home, part time and full time; I have

1 Victoria Richards, 'I Felt Lost In Motherhood. Here's How I Reclaimed My Identity', *The Huffington Post*, 1 February 2020, huffingtonpost.co.uk.

volunteered, and I have been self-employed and employed. When our children were small and I was at home full time, my husband Richard and I were invited to a smart dinner. In my life BC (before children) I would have looked forward to the evening – a chance to dress up, enjoy good food and meet some interesting people, and I would have accepted the invitation immediately. However, in this new season things had changed, and I found myself approaching the evening with some trepidation. The prospect of arranging a babysitter who could put four children to bed, then squeezing my body into my BC dress were the first two hurdles to overcome. These, however, paled into insignificance in comparison with my anxiety about whether I would be able to engage in interesting conversation, or even have the ability to string a coherent sentence together about anything other than the escaped hamster, the new recipe for Play-Doh or my daughter's new reading book. My fears were not unfounded. Once pre-dinner drinks were successfully negotiated, we were shown to our places. Seated to my right was a media guru and to my left a business consultant. As we sat down, the consultant turned to me and asked me the question I had been dreading:

'Do you work?'

I mumbled something about being at home with the children then he gave me a kind smile and turned his attention to the lady on his left, with whom I imagine he had a much more interesting conversation. Years later I came across a brilliant answer given by another mother when asked the same question:

Yes ... I'm in a programme of social development. At the moment I'm working with three age groups. First, with babies and toddlers. That involves a basic grasp of medicine and child psychology. Next ... teenagers. I confess the programme is not going so well in that area. Finally, at evenings and weekends, I work with a man aged thirty-nine who is exhibiting all the classic symptoms of mid-life crisis. That's mainly psychiatric work. The whole job involves planning, a 'make-it-happen' attitude and the ability to crisis-manage.[2]

With a smile, she added, 'I used to be an international lawyer, but I got bored!'

If only I'd had this answer then – I'd have given him something to consult about!

There is a wonderful scene in the Disney film *The Lion King*. Simba's wicked uncle, Scar, has tricked the young lion into thinking he is responsible for the death of his father, Mufasa, the king. Grief-stricken, Simba flees into exile and leaves behind his identity as the Lion King. Rafiki the mandrill befriends him and seeking to restore him to the throne, takes him to meet with the spirit of his father. In a reflection from a pool, Mufasa's voice booms from the deep as he speaks to his son, 'Simba, remember who you are.'[3]

2 Rob and Dianne Parsons, *The Sixty Minute Mother talks to Rob Parsons*, Hodder, 2000, p49.
3 *The Lion King*, directed by Roger Allers and Rob Minkoff, Walt Disney Pictures, 1994.

Remember who you are.

As parents, we would do well to do the same. We have an identity not defined by our roles in the workplace or by our role as partners or parents, important as those are. We are unique individuals with different gifts and needs, each of whom has been placed on Planet Earth for a purpose. In the turmoil and busyness of family life, particularly in the early days, it's well worth taking just a few moments to … remember who you are.

THERE'S NO POINT TRYING TO BE A SUPERHERO

I put the finishing touches to the birthday cake and glanced at the kitchen clock. It was thirty-five minutes past midnight. I stood back to admire my handiwork and had to admit that it was a masterpiece. Rows of miniature coloured-icing carrots, radishes, French beans and lettuces were planted in the chocolate icing vegetable patch. A wheelbarrow and garden fork stood nearby, alongside the scarecrow wearing Peter Rabbit's blue jacket and shoes hung there by Mr McGregor. Beatrix Potter herself would have been proud. Everything would be perfect for Charlotte's birthday party.

Years later my friends still laugh about 'The Peter Rabbit cake'. It has gone down in the annals of our friendship, but not for the reasons I would have hoped. The cake incident might possibly have been overlooked if my efforts to rival *The Great British Bake Off* had stopped there. But they didn't. I am embarrassed to admit that I recently discovered a photograph album of Hill family themed birthday cakes – Thunderbirds, princesses, castles, forts, dinosaurs, a Mad Hatter's top hat (the pièce de résistance for an *Alice in Wonderland* themed party complete with fancy dress), boats, cars, pirate chests and many more works of art besides. Apparently, in my efforts to create a centrepiece to remember, I had inadvertently raised the bar and condemned my friends to attempt to do likewise – including creations of Mickey Mouse, the Starship Enterprise and more Ninja Turtles than any of them were inclined to remember.

We laugh about it now, but looking back, I can see that this cake represented my attempt to be Supermum. I needed to face the uncomfortable truth and ask myself what I was trying to prove, who I was trying to impress, and who the Peter Rabbit cake and others like it were really for. It certainly wasn't for the four-year-olds at the party, who would have been just as happy with a caterpillar cake from Tesco.

It seems that I am not alone. A recent report shows that the average parent posts almost 1,500 images of their child before their fifth birthday.[4] Scrolling down, Emily's starring role as a raindrop in the nativity play is followed by Alfie's spectacular dive that nearly saved the match and many other proud parent moments besides. Two-thirds of parents said they use social media to post status updates about their offspring, and over half the parents who were polled admitted they were most likely to use social media to boast about their child's achievements. Family life is full of special moments that it is good to celebrate and enjoy, but before we hit the 'share' button it might be worth taking a moment to check our motives.

What can feel like the relentless pressure to achieve as a parent can result in us seeking to wear our underpants outside our trousers. Many parents struggle to strike a balance between work and home, feeling the pressure to excel in both areas, and the Covid-19 pandemic brought this into sharp focus. *Forbes* magazine wrote in 2021:

4 Security.org Report, 'Parents' Social Media Habits: 2021', *security.org*, 13 May 2021, security.org.

Being a working parent was already a difficult place to be. With the arrival of Covid-19, and the subsequent shift to remote work and the economic downturn that followed, working parents, especially working mothers, were faced with even greater challenges.[5]

Being a parent is one of the most important and challenging roles that we can have and deserves our very best efforts. But we need to dispel once and for all the myth that we need to be a superhero. Parenting is not a competition, and we can be free of the pressure to perform.

5 Ashley Stahl, 'Struggles for Working Parents are Likely to Remain post-Pandemic', *Forbes Magazine*, 2 April 2021.

Let's lay down the comparisons, be real about both the joys and the challenges, decide how we want to parent in our particular family situation – and then simply do our best. We have nothing to prove.

Superhero parents

 Always have all the stuff for a morning of junk modelling

 Always return library books several days early

 Always redeem supermarket coupons before the expiry date

 Always know the school holiday dates

 Always get to the bottom of the ironing basket

 Always wash PE kit every Friday night

 Always co-ordinate lifts for their children and their friends to lots of extracurricular activities

 Always provide beautiful homemade cupcakes for the school bazaar

 Never lose track of how much screen time their children have had in a day

 Never double-book themselves for parents' evening and …

 … are never, ever late on the school run!

LAY DOWN
THE GUILT

I have had the privilege of speaking with thousands of parents over the years – they have shared with me their joys, fears, hopes and aspirations for their children. But time and time again they confide this: they feel guilty.

These parents are not serial offenders; most haven't got skeletons lying in the cupboard under the stairs. No, they are ordinary parents who are tired – not so much of doing the main task of parenting but of feeling that they are failing. One put it like this: 'Every time I hear an expert give a "foolproof" way to deal with the kids, I find that mine are the exception to the rule!'

And the school gate can be a scary place for the parent not up-to-date with the latest idea. Livy, mother to six-year-old Josh, said:

'While I love chatting with my friends at pick up time, and sharing our parenting experiences, sometimes the different advice can feel overwhelming. A few weeks ago I realized Josh was behind with his reading, and I decided I needed to push him a bit more. Then another parent told me that was the worst thing I could do, saying, "You'll kill his love of books!"'

Poor Livy went on to say that it wasn't just reading – it was screen time, sugar, vitamins, gaming, exercise, bedtimes – going back to work, child care, managing her children's and her own wellbeing and a hundred other things besides.

All these things caused guilt. 'At times my head whirls with it all,' she said.

I want to share a secret with you: when it comes to their own children, there are no experts. The people who write the books, the ones who appear in the media or podcasts or give advice in magazines – all of them are just people trying to get their own children through as best they can. So above all, have confidence in your own parenting.

Nobody knows your child like you – and nobody loves them like you. There is no one way to be a perfect parent – but there are a hundred ways to be a great parent.

Nobody sums up this issue of guilt better than a mother who wrote in to Care for the Family:

> Mother guilt is attached to the umbilical cord,
> but it stays with you for life.
> You feel guilty about what you do
> and guilty about what you don't do.
> Guilty when you leave them
> and guilty when you pick them up.
> Guilty about what they eat,
> what they don't eat
> and even what they might eat.
> The guilt gets you at night,
> on the train,
> standing in the school playground
> and especially when you've left them to have a break.
> Then it usually gets attached to your purse
> and leads you to a toyshop.
> What mothers need
> is a jury of twelve good mothers and true
> to stand up and say
> 'Not guilty m'lud'.[6]

The time when I most needed to hear that 'not guilty' verdict was on a memorable half-term trip to London some years ago …

6 Rob and Dianne Parsons, *The Sixty Minute Mother talks to Rob Parsons*, Hodder, 2000, p99.

As we walked to the car, the children trailed behind, kicking the last of the autumn leaves on the pavement. I took a moment to enjoy the scene, patted myself on the back, and enjoyed a rare moment of pride in my parental prowess. As family days out go, this had been a good one. My husband Richard and I had navigated all four children around the steamy tropical rainforests of the Natural History Museum, getting up close to dinosaurs, earthquakes and volcanoes, and then to cap it all had hopped on and off the District and Circle line without major incident. I felt well pleased.

We had parked our car near the Tube station for an easy getaway. I knew that by 5pm blood sugars would be running low, and I was anxious to get everyone back for tea. As I unlocked the car, the warm glow of satisfaction quickly began to fade. Son number one apparently had dog poo on his shoe, and his siblings were refusing to get into the car with him. I issued an ultimatum – 'If you don't stop arguing and get into the car, you will have to walk home.'

Everyone climbed in and off we set. After about five minutes of sitting in rush hour traffic George (eight) asked a question destined to put fear into the heart of even the most laid-back parent. 'Where's Charlotte?'

At first I thought he was joking – in our hurry to get home coats had been thrown on the floor of the car and I imagined she was hiding under them. But no – in a heart-stopping moment we realized she wasn't in the car. We had left her standing on the pavement in the middle of London. She was six years old. In blind panic, ignoring the protests of London taxis and rush hour commuters, we made a U-turn and headed back to where we had parked the car. It seemed to take an eternity. She was nowhere to be seen. I jumped out and ran up and down the neighbouring roads. I remember taking the steps of the station bridge two at a time, and looking wildly out across the common. She was wearing a red hoodie and in the fading light everywhere seemed to be little girls wearing red, but none were Charlotte. At that moment my husband started tooting the car horn madly to get my attention – he had seen her disappearing down the adjacent street, but couldn't get to her because of the traffic. Running faster than I had ever run before, I caught up with her and scooped her up. Tears of relief flowed. It wasn't until later that evening we discovered the back-story. In protest at being told to sit next to her brother she had stormed off down the road, fully expecting us to pick her up. What she had failed to notice was that the car was facing in the opposite direction. I hadn't taken a roll call, assumed everyone was on board and we had driven off without her.

The emotion of that twenty minutes will stay with me forever: in fact even revisiting it now makes my stomach churn. I have often thought how the outcome could have been so different, and have rehearsed in my mind the conversation I might have had with an officer from the London Met, as I explained that I had told my six-year-old daughter to walk home and had driven off leaving her behind. Parental guilt comes with the umbilical cord – and as a mother, this was one of the most guilt-inducing moments of my life.

When we feel we have really messed up, the guilt can be hard to bear. As well as beating ourselves up, we sometimes add insult to injury by comparing ourselves to parents who (from the outside at least) seem to have perfect children. They save their pocket money for study guides, self-regulate screen time, and offer to help with the washing-up because 'you've had a hard day at work.' I imagine if my children fitted into this category I might be tempted to do the same, but these parents make the mistake of taking all the credit for their children's 'success' and encourage others to follow their example, readily sharing their top tips and advice. If that happens to be you:

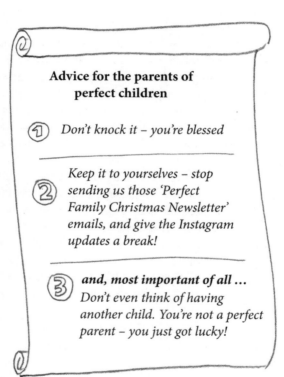

Advice for the parents of perfect children

1. *Don't knock it – you're blessed*

2. *Keep it to yourselves – stop sending us those 'Perfect Family Christmas Newsletter' emails, and give the Instagram updates a break!*

3. ***and, most important of all …*** *Don't even think of having another child. You're not a perfect parent – you just got lucky!*

CHILDREN WILL BE AS DIFFERENT AS CHALK AND CHEESE

In the weeks before our third child was born, I remember wondering which of the other two children he would be like – and then being surprised afterwards to discover that he was different again!

Our children are unique, and if we have more than one child, we may well discover that they are completely different in temperament. And if we are the parent of just one child, we will also soon discover how different they are to their peers. One may be challenging, the other compliant, and others a whole range of temperaments in between.

Rob Parsons, the chairman and founder of Care for the Family, often speaks about the differences between his two children, Katie and Lloyd. Katie was the first, and she was a typical compliant child. Rob writes:

The first thing Katie did when she came into the world was to apologise to the midwife for being a little late ... Dianne and I thought we were the perfect parents. We tutted to each other as we watched other toddlers having tantrums in the aisles of supermarkets. Sometimes, with hardly concealed glee, we pointed out to other parents where they might be going wrong with their offspring. And then Lloyd came into our lives ... The parenting gurus tell us that if your first child is shy, careful and compliant, your second will be different. Lloyd was desperate not to disappoint those experts.[7]

In contrast, for Richard and I it was our first child who was born with the determination to test boundaries at all costs, just to make sure they were really there. I used to look at other parents with children who agreed to wear their coats, kept the water in the bath, ate their broccoli and didn't kick their siblings, and ask myself, 'Where have I gone wrong?'

The truth was, I hadn't. Children are born with different temperaments, and, try as we might, it is not our task as parents to change them. Of course, I wanted to teach our son to have good qualities, such as being kind and thinking of others, but it is his outlook on life that has enabled him to grow into a fun-loving, bright young man who lights up a room, isn't afraid to challenge the status quo, and has a heart for justice. (And now he even eats broccoli!)

Another of our boys was born with a fiercely competitive spirit, which made even a game of tiddlywinks a challenge. Losing, in his mind, is for losers. In the early days I tried to change this trait in him. If his team lost at football I would remind him that it was only a game. But my words seemed to fall on deaf ears. I have come now to understand that winning is always going to be important to him. It's the way he is wired. Of course I wanted to teach him to lose (and to win) graciously. During his childhood, losing a game of tennis would invariably result in outbursts that put the best of Wimbledon centre court dramas in the shade. So we would try to encourage him to remain calm and to congratulate his opponent at the end of the

7 Rob and Dianne Parsons, *The Sixty Minute Mother talks to Rob Parsons*, Hodder, 2000, pp94–95 and p8.

match – even if it was between gritted teeth. Similarly, when the score was in his favour, we suggested he toned down the victory lap around the court. It was an area he needed to work on, but if channelled well, that competitive edge is what gives him the focus and determination to persevere and succeed.

Our children's individual personalities and temperaments will determine how they build relationships and make friends. I remember noticing this on a family holiday. Having set up camp with all the paraphernalia needed for a family day at the beach, our children began happily paddling in a stream. They were soon joined by two other children and played with them until lunchtime, building dams and constructing a system of waterworks that would have made Defra proud.

23

When our daughter returned to where we were sitting she told us all about her new best friend, Lucy. Lucy lived in London, she had two brothers, a new kitten, a hamster, a goldfish, a pink bedroom and a new butterfly hairclip. Her class teacher next term would be Mrs Webster. They were friends forever.

Her brother returned a few minutes later. As no information from him was forthcoming, I enquired about the new friend he'd been digging alongside for the past few hours. He looked puzzled, paused for a moment and then said,

'Oh him … he's just a boy.'

For the boys, activity had been the centre of their relationship; they were perfectly happy digging together and not engaging in any conversation. In contrast, the girls had earnestly exchanged the minutiae of life in both their families.

I remember commenting to my husband that whereas Charlotte followed me all around the house chatting constantly, it was hard to get so much as a syllable out of one of our sons.

Richard grunted and said, 'Mmm.'

Exactly!

Our children's unique personalities mean that they are likely to be as different as chalk and cheese. Let's celebrate the differences in their temperaments, look for the positives, and encourage the qualities that in later life will enable them to make a difference in the world.

Let's be the wind at their backs and encourage them to be the people that they were made to be.

DON'T LOOK SIDEWAYS

The first time I ventured out solo in my parents' car after having passed my driving test, I had been driving for about ten minutes when I came to a narrow stretch of road between two parked cars. Having not been blessed with any sense of spatial awareness, I had no idea if I could fit through. A queue of traffic soon built up behind as I inched forward, causing all the A-type personality commuters whose sorry fate it was to be behind me a dangerous rise in blood pressure. Sweating profusely, I inched forward with no idea how I was going to negotiate that gap. I had read *The Highway Code* from cover to cover, but I could not remember it giving any advice or guidance for this situation.

As I veered terrifyingly close to the parked cars, the passenger door came within an inch of its life. The driver in the car behind me could contain herself no longer and jumped out to come to my rescue. She stood in front of my car and began walking backwards, gesticulating madly. 'Eyes straight ahead,' she shouted. 'Don't look sideways, look at me!' This woman was my saviour. As I focussed ahead rather than on the parked cars to the sides, I found I could drive safely through the gap without inflicting any scrapes or marks on my parents' car or the two cars on either side.

I later reflected that not only was this an excellent lesson about driving, but also for life itself. As a parent, I so often gave in to the temptation to take my eye off the destination and to look sideways – to make a comparison. It only resulted in feelings of discouragement in the belief that others were doing a better job than me.

The two hours between 10am and 12 noon on a Sunday were when these thoughts would be uppermost in my mind. Getting everyone dressed and out of the door in time for the 10am service was always a Herculean task. We would invariably scuttle in as the first hymn was announced, only to find ourselves sitting behind Mrs M and her three beautifully behaved children who had, of course, taken their seats well before the start of the service. Keeping our four under control felt more like refereeing a wrestling match than engaging in morning worship. The antics in our row were in sharp contrast to the goings-on in front, where the family M children, with shiny shoes and blonde pigtails, would sit quietly and give the appearance of listening attentively throughout. Hardly a week would go by without Mrs M turning around to smile and say what became familiar words, 'Goodness! You've got your hands full.'

No doubt she meant well, but the comment did nothing to encourage us in our ability to parent with confidence. While centile charts are useful for monitoring our children's growth and development, and comparethemarket.com may help us land the best deal for car or travel insurance, comparison is not a good tool to keep in the toolbox of parenting.

One parent put it like this:

'It's so easy to look sideways and feel that everybody else is doing a much better job than you, and then to feel bad. When other people's children come to visit they are so polite – and I am genuinely surprised when other parents tell me that mine are too, when they visit them. I spend half my life hoping my

kids won't give the game away about what I'm really like as a mother – but I'm giving it my best shot and we're doing fine.'

There is of course much we can learn as parents, and it's good to share stories and experiences and to encourage others who are at the same life stage. But the ancient book of Proverbs gives good advice:

Let your eyes look directly forward, and your gaze be straight before you.[8]

That advice got me through my driving career without too many scrapes, and it can protect the bodywork of parents too.

8 Proverbs 4:25–26, ESV.

ASK
YOURSELF:
'WHAT
DOES A
GOOD JOB
REALLY
LOOK
LIKE'

Ask yourself:
'What does a good job really *look like?'*

Like many couples, Richard and I have different approaches to parenting, and I have often had to moderate my natural tendency to want to be in control.

Bedtime routine would be where this would sometimes come to the fore. Getting four children upstairs, bathed, pyjamas on, teeth cleaned, stories read and into bed required the strategic know-how and planning of a military campaign. Maybe it was because I had often been with the children all day, but by 7pm I just wanted to get them settled and into bed – no high-jinks or other antics – and I had the routine down to a fine art. Richard would invariably arrive halfway through the proceedings. Fun with his children was a highlight at the end of the day – and he would invariably have games galore up his sleeve, which usually involved lots of shrieking and running around or bouncing on beds. My irritation at his hijacking of the bedtime routine would often focus on the lack of supervision given to teeth cleaning. The children would all clean their teeth – but not in the way that I thought it should be done. Richard simply did not seem able to grasp the required amount of horizontal and vertical brushes that are needed to instruct a six-year-old in dental hygiene. On more than one occasion I found myself taking over. But the honest truth is that I was going over the top.

By the time our fourth came along, I would hardly worry if the poor soul was soaking his dentures in the bath. And at some point along the way I remembered a question that I asked in workplace appraisals: 'What does a good job look like?'

In hindsight, I am sure Richard's toothbrushing supervision was more than adequate (all four still have their teeth as young adults!), but my inner belief that only my way was best often led to him backing off.

We would do well to lay down perfectionism, and to realize that good enough generally is good enough.

And if you are parenting alone, take all the help you can get, from grandparents, other family members, neighbours and friends. If they aren't doing the job exactly as you would, before jumping in to set them right, press the pause button and ask yourself, 'What does a good job *really* look like?'

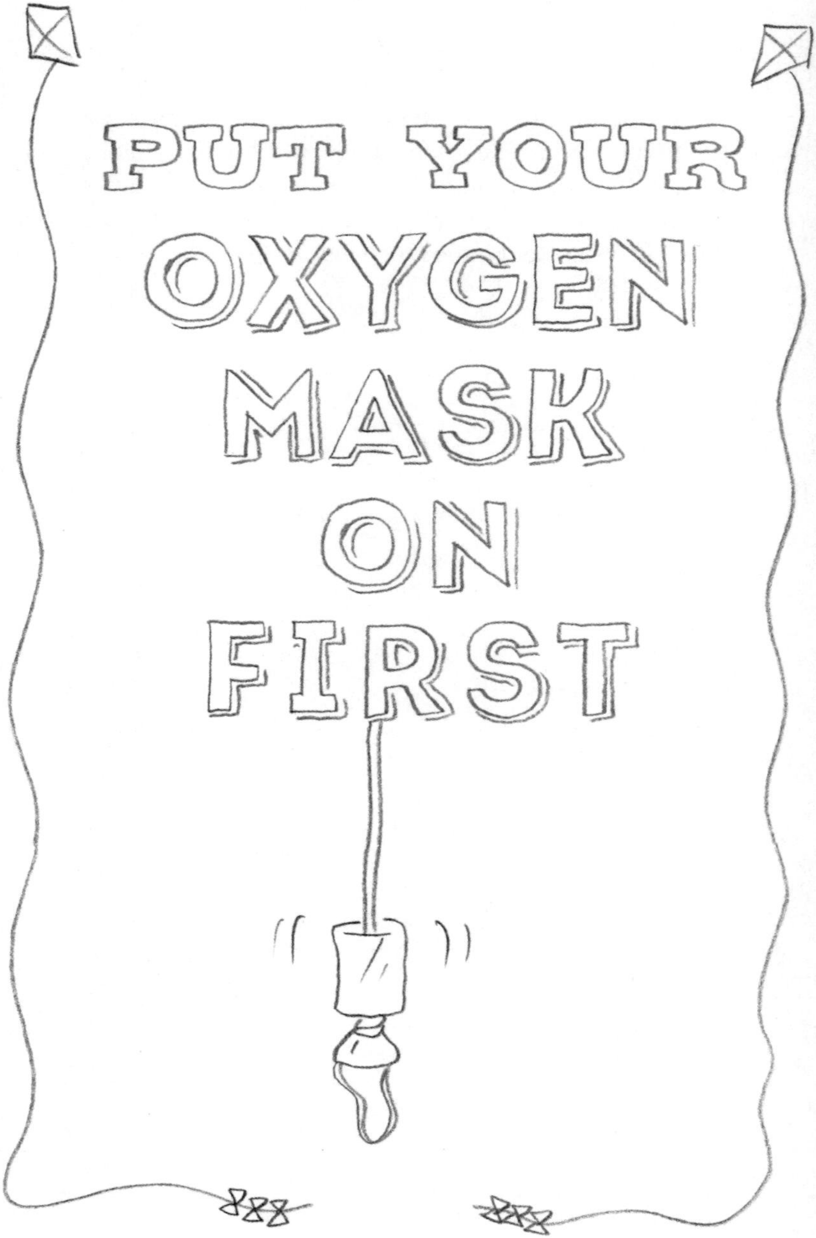
PUT YOUR
OXYGEN
MASK
ON
FIRST

Put your oxygen mask on first

Many of us will be familiar with the aircraft safety announcement telling people to ensure they put their own oxygen masks on first before attending to their children. This direction may sound counterintuitive for parents, but attending to our own needs first in an emergency means we are better able to help our children.

So many things cause us stress as parents. Statistics published at the beginning of 2020 revealed that an estimated one in six adults had experienced a 'common mental disorder' in the past week[9] and since then we have experienced the Covid-19 pandemic. A recent survey of its impact on adults suggests that anxiety, depression, loneliness and self-harm are intensifying.[10] Although scientists have yet to find a single anxiety gene, our temperament undoubtedly makes a big difference to how we handle stress and anxiety. I'm not generally an anxious person, but whenever there are issues in my children's lives that I'm helpless to control, my fears skyrocket.

If you are struggling physically or emotionally, don't keep this to yourself. Talk with trusted friends and family, and seek professional support if needed. Seeing you address your own struggles in a constructive way is both reassuring for your children and sets a good pattern for them to follow.

As parents, our heartfelt desire to do the very best for our children can be all-consuming. If we are not careful, the result

9 Carl Baker, 'Mental Health Statistics for England: Prevalence, Services and Funding', *House of Commons Briefing Paper no. 6988*, 23 January 2020, parliament.uk.
10 Libby Brooks, 'Concern for Britons feeling trapped and lonely during lockdown', *The Guardian*, 19 April 2020, guardian.com.

of pouring ourselves totally into their lives can be that we neglect to look after ourselves or fail to make time to invest in important adult relationships.

When our youngest started school, Richard suggested that we asked a friend to come to stay so that we could go away for a night, just the two of us. His observation was that we had got into a rut of only ever talking about the children. He wanted time away when, just for a moment, we could forget the relentlessness of family responsibilities, and have fun together, like we used to BC (before children). He had a voucher for a hotel in Wales set in a beautiful valley surrounded by rolling hills. The restaurant promised delicious, locally sourced food that put our routine family meals of sausages, fish fingers or pasta into the shade. It sounded such a lovely idea.

But to Richard's disappointment, I said 'No.' My reluctance was rooted in the fact that I felt we would, in some way, be letting our children down by leaving them behind for twenty-four hours. In hindsight I realize how wrong I was. In these early years we found the demands of family life meant that we were only giving each other the dregs of our time at the end of the day. We had long to-do lists in the evening: homework to be supervised, spellings to be learnt, lifts to be given, meals to be prepared, sports kits to be washed, children to be bathed, stories to be read, and bedtime to be negotiated. The mantra we adopted – 'divide and conquer' – worked well. We would decide who was going to be responsible for which task and set about doing them in parallel – Richard would be in one part of the house, working through his list and I would be in another. But while that may work for getting through all the evening chores before midnight, it is not a good habit to adopt long term. Fortunately, good sense later prevailed, and we did eventually enjoy a night away on our own. It was one of the best investments of time we ever made. We realized that it was important that we made time for each other – not just in things like an occasional night away, which is not always possible, but in small ways. It always involved a little planning and the help of others, but to us it became a lifeline.

If you are parenting as a couple, avoid slipping into 'parallel living' by looking out for opportunities for things you can do together. Some wise friends encouraged us to put a 'date night' into the diary each week. This date doesn't have to be complicated or even cost money. Our first 'outing' on our own was to walk to the local pub for a drink, although some more imaginative ones followed, including a closely fought game of crazy golf. It was simply a time away from the humdrum demands of family life,

to focus on each other, have fun and talk – to put on that oxygen mask for the week ahead.

One of the advantages of the primary years is that you can (in theory!) have some time after the children are in bed. Make the most of it – the teenage years when they are up and about all evening will be here before you know it! To save on getting a babysitter, we have had many date nights at home. The deal was that there was to be no checking of emails, folding of washing, DIY jobs or other household chores but simply time together. Sometimes we lit a candle and cooked a nice meal, watched a film or simply chatted over a glass of wine. For a number of years we were able to seize a 'date night' moment during the day, and would grab a coffee while the children were at school. Find the time that works best for you. It may involve being both flexible and creative but generally where there's a will, there's a way!

It has been said that the best thing a father can do for his children is to love their mother, and of course, that works the other way round as well. There are obviously other reasons for investing in our couple relationship, but the fact that it benefits our children is not a bad place to start. For many it is not easy, but if you possibly can, think about going on a marriage course – a kind of MOT for your relationship. We went on one when our children were in the primary years and it was one of the best investments we could have made.

If you are parenting on your own, it's equally important to give time to adult relationships that energize you. Through our Care for the Family events, I meet a lot of single parents. Many feel isolated and alone, and anything we can do to ease that burden can be life-changing. One mother spoke of the difficulties she faced:

'Twenty-four-hour parenting – there's no one else when you've just had enough. Even ordinary things can seem like mountains to climb. I'm scared of getting flu because somebody has to care for my kids. The other day I had to go into hospital for a minor operation, but first I had to get somebody to have my two children for a couple of days. You'd think it would be easy, but sometimes it seems impossible ... [Money is] ... often hand to mouth ... we don't have much. I don't care so much about myself, but I want them to have what other kids have. There's just nobody to talk to. Nobody to say, "Don't be daft" or "Let the baby cry for a while" or "You're doing a great job." I so often have the sense that I really am on my own.'[11]

My heart went out to this mother. I know it's not always possible, but if we can find others to share with, it will make a big difference. And perhaps those of us who have friends who are parenting alone can try to go the second mile to be there for them.

Jill, a single parent with two young children, said:

'My other adult friends have been a lifeline to me. I have to fight for the time, but it's worth it. I've discovered I'm a much better parent to my kids when I've had some adult company. It helps me keep a sense of perspective and stops everything getting on top of me.'

As well as the pressures of family life, there are other factors that can cause us stress and anxiety. Fears we already have about the state of the world into which we have brought our children can be fuelled by 24/7 news stories of war and terrorism, climate change, knife crime, grooming and child abduction not to

11 Rob and Dianne Parsons, *The Sixty Minute Mother talks to Rob Parsons*, Hodder, 2000, pp65–66.

mention the effect of the Covid-19 pandemic on our children's mental wellbeing. Ironically, worrying about their children's anxiety is one of the most common reasons parents give for having sleepless nights themselves.[12] Little eyes are watching and little ears are listening, and if we are feeling anxious it is all too easy to pass our anxiety on to our children. Part of putting on that oxygen mask first will therefore involve prioritizing our own emotional wellbeing. Find ways to relax and recharge – turn off your phone, and grab a few quiet moments, have a deep bath, listen to your favourite music, have coffee with a friend, go for a run – whatever works for you.

Finding time to look after our own wellbeing is vital, not just for our sakes, but for the sake of our children. The oxygen mask will drop down from a panel above your seat – remember to put it on first and everyone will benefit.

12 Alicia Eaton, *First Aid for Your Child's Mind*, Practical Inspiration Publishing, 2019, p10.

LISTENING SAYS: 'YOU MATTER'

I was recently invited to a networking event for women. I was pleased to have received the invitation as there was a particular guest that I was keen to meet. I had admired her for some time, and felt sure I would have lots to learn from her experience. I arrived and made my way into the room, which was already full. The organizer greeted me and introduced me to a group of people, which included the person I was keen to connect with. I couldn't believe my good fortune. We began talking, but before too long I became aware that her attention was not on me, but on a conversation going on just behind my left shoulder. I battled on for a few minutes and then stepped aside so she could join the other group. Her distraction and failure to listen made me feel insignificant and invisible, and I soon made my apologies and left the gathering. However many pearls of wisdom she may have shared with me at a later time, her inability to listen and to engage with me rendered them worthless.

This was in sharp contrast to a friend I called on in a moment of need. Looking back, I realize that it wasn't a great time to have just dropped in on her, unannounced. She had recently started her own business and was up to her eyes in admin. But somehow she sensed my need. She closed the laptop, looked into my eyes and said, 'Tell me about it.' And I did. I will always remember the feeling of worth and value that she gave me when she put her work to one side and simply listened.

As parents, we have the same power at our disposal. We can make our children feel valued and special, just by listening. Our youngest loved animals, and had declared on more than one occasion that when he grew up he wanted to be a vet. I remember him saying to me one day, 'I think my hamster is having babies.'

It was 7pm in the evening and I had been in my new job for exactly two days and was trying to wade through the office manual that made *War and Peace* look like a pamphlet. I ignored him.

I felt reasonably justified in this for two reasons: firstly, said hamster had been alone in the cage for as long as we had owned it; secondly 'Spike' was male. So if Spike had somehow managed this feat, then both Henry and I were going to make a lot of money.

I didn't take my eyes off 'Employees' responsibilities on noticing breaches of IT procedures' and said, 'Not now, darling – later.'

Usually children are content with the 'We'll do it later' routine – they believe us and we believe ourselves as we are saying it. But sometimes 'later' is not good enough. When I saw his face I knew that this was one of those moments.

We can't always do it – we probably shouldn't always do it – but the truth is that so often it doesn't take much time to make a child feel not only listened to, but special. On this occasion – although alas, not on every one – I chose well. I laid down the manual and heard myself say, 'Well, darling, that is amazing – now where is that book on hamsters we bought?'

Another time, our daughter Charlotte, who was about five, had just returned from a friend's house, where she had seen an exciting film. It had a complicated plot involving an ice queen, an enchanted wood, a hummingbird, a knight, a castle, and a lengthy cast list besides. As we sat around the kitchen table, she began to tell us the story, unravelling the plot frame by frame and in excruciating detail. It was incredibly boring and my concentration started to wander. My eyes fell on a magazine article next to me on the table with the headline '10 Ways to Declutter Your Home'. Our home was in dire need of a Marie Kondo makeover at that point, so I read the first few lines and was immediately hooked. Charlotte continued for a while without missing a beat, but then she stopped.

'Mummy, you're not listening.'

'Yes, I am darling,' I said, while wondering where on earth the author stored her papers in her minimalist home.

'No, you're not, Mummy. You need to listen with your eyes.'

She was right. I had completely disengaged with the exploits of the ice queen and the hummingbird, but, more so, I had disengaged with my daughter. Listening to our children means turning off the running dialogue in our head, switching off our phone, pausing our to-do list and giving our children our full attention.

The challenge is that we see the world through adult eyes. The things we think are important are often not so high on our children's agenda. Listening generally means stopping what we are doing – finishing that email, checking our phone, chopping that onion, or emptying the dishwasher – and gives the message, 'You matter.' When our children are small, kneeling down, perhaps cupping their face in our hands and giving them eye contact as they describe their drawing of the cat or the model dinosaur they made out of junk, conveys to them that we are interested in them, that they are important to us.[13] Parents who have children with additional needs will need to discover what works for them in this regard, as their children might struggle with receiving touch, listening, paying attention, eye contact and other nonverbal cues. Each situation will be different, but as a parent, you will be the expert on your own child.

13 S.K. Singh, 'Family Communication', *Global Journal of Arts and Management*, 2011, pp11–13.

IT'S GOOD TO TALK

Our son had just moved up to junior school, and it was about three weeks into term. He arrived in our bedroom in his pyjamas one Tuesday morning to say he wasn't well – he had been sick – and so wouldn't be able to go to school. He took me to the bathroom to show me the evidence, and sure enough the loo was full of what looked decidedly like vomit. However, I couldn't help doubting the truth of the story as this child looked the picture of health. My suspicions were confirmed when I went downstairs for breakfast and found a newly opened packet of muesli. Shreddies or Rice Krispies were his cereals of choice. He didn't like nuts and made a huge fuss if there was a raisin in his bowl – I knew he wouldn't have touched muesli. And the penny dropped. Muesli, masquerading as sick, had been jettisoned down the loo. In fact, so convincing was it, that son number one had been within an inch of pulling the wool over his mother's eyes and securing a day off school. I let him know in no uncertain terms how mad I was with him not just for the original escapade but also for lying. We were already late, so I packed him off to school with his tail between his legs.

It was only later that evening that I took the time to allow him to talk and the whole story came tumbling out. Sometimes our children are just being naughty, but on this occasion I realized that my son had been trying to tell me something – and

I hadn't really been listening. Tuesday was swimming day, and he had been put in a swimming class that was too difficult for him. He had been so anxious about it that he had staged the muesli episode so he wouldn't have to go. Having discovered the truth, I was able to see the swimming teacher who arranged for him to be moved to a lower class the following week.

Life is busy and it is not always possible, but looking back I could have saved that child a great deal of angst and heartache if only I had spotted the cues he was giving me. They may not be ready to or even want to share their hearts with us, but at least we can give them the opportunity. Try allowing a moment – in the car, at bedtime, after a meal – just to allow space to talk.

It's important to try to understand the feelings behind our children's words or behaviour. Amir is a compliant child, but his mother, Sadia, was recently called into school by his teacher to talk about his bad behaviour. A few days later at bedtime, she took a moment to ask him how his day had been. 'I hate school,' he said, then shut his eyes. Sadia decided not to leave  it there. As she gently asked a few more questions, the story tumbled out. A few weeks earlier, Amir had got up from his chair and just as another child was about to sit on it, a classmate said, 'Don't sit on Amir's chair. You'll get a disease.' Since then, he'd been living with anger, hurt and anxiety bottled up inside.

After talking with his mother and getting things off his chest, Amir left for school in a much better frame of mind and fortunately it proved to be a one-off incident. Not every problem will be so easily resolved, but listening out for how our children are feeling and prompting them to share their thoughts with us is often a catalyst that enables them to move on.

Those 'muesli moments' occur in all our lives – times when we are scared, worried or confused. As adults, we often learn to hide them, but just as taking the time to talk them through with a friend can help us, with our children it's important that we give them the time and space just to talk.

Our children are growing up in an anxious world and in our digital age we can't shield them from distressing news reports as global events unfold. We may have put the news on in the background while we're cooking tea, perhaps forgetting that our children are watching and taking it all in. And even if our children aren't accessing reports on social media, they will almost certainly be getting information from friends.

As parents we may be feeling overwhelmed, struggling to find words to make sense of what is happening on the world stage ourselves, let alone being able to talk about it to our children. But talk to them we must. Depending on their personality our children may respond differently – but an escalating crisis in Europe or reports of irreversible climate change will undoubtedly lead to feelings of uncertainty, anxiety and fear that need to be unpacked. As parents, we are best placed to do that. Rather than one big talk, a much better method is to try to introduce the subject in an everyday context – while doing Lego, cleaning out the rabbit, or at meal times. And although it's important to explain things appropriately to our children, it's also OK to admit sometimes that we don't have all the answers.

Rather than overwhelming our children with too much information, we can ask open questions and then listen to what their concerns really are. Sometimes the issues bothering them won't be what we expect. A friend who thought she should speak to her son about Covid-19 prepared a science lesson that would have given Einstein a run for his money. It turned out that rather than having questions about the virus itself, he was troubled about a much more mundane issue – not being able to go to the cake shop after school.

And we can try to 'listen for their feelings'. Even if we think they're worrying about something insignificant, rather than a dismissive, 'Don't worry,' acknowledging how they feel – 'I see you are worried' – will make them feel valued and understood.

Love them and let them know

Rockleaze Rangers football club provided the opportunity for a release of pent-up energy for our three boys and their friends, (and a freezing ninety minutes on the sideline for us parents) every Saturday morning during the football season. This club was wonderfully well-run by a group of dads, who were our heroes. The time, energy and organization that they invested in the club rivalled the Premier League. Fitness was encouraged, team formations were planned, league games completed and tournaments arranged against rival clubs. The focus of the year, however, was the end of season Award Ceremony in the school hall. Coca-Cola and crisps were laid on, with awards for every achievement imaginable – most improved player, best goal scored, best goal saved, best tackle, and best team player, to name but a few. But the trophy that every child dreamed of winning was 'Player of the Year.'

Ed had played well that year – he had made it to the first team and scored the winning goal in the tournament – we knew he was in with a good chance. The only other contender was his friend Alfie, but Alfie had won Player of the Year the year before and hadn't scored the winning goal, so we were pretty confident Ed would be walking home with the trophy held high that evening. As the evening drew to a climax, the tension mounted. Ed was in the front row with his mates, who were as confident as he was of the result. The manager stepped forward and made the announcement: Player of the Year would go … not to Ed Hill or even Alfie Harris, but to Dan Smith, a complete outsider.

While our task that night was to console a disappointed eight-year-old, in the weeks to come it also gave the opportunity to teach him an important life lesson. The world gives our children the message that they are loved and accepted when they are successful and do well. But as parents, we have the opportunity to give them a different message. Whether or not they come top in the spelling test, are picked for the netball team, get a good part in the play or even win Rockleaze Rangers' Player of the Year award, we have the opportunity to show them that our love for them isn't based on what they achieve, but on who they are. The most precious gift we can give our children is the knowledge that they are loved anyway.

It's as if each child has an emotional tank inside them that is crying out to be filled with love. Just as the petrol gauge on the car shows how much fuel is in the tank, our children's behaviour is often the gauge that shows us how full their 'emotional tank' is – how loved they feel.

Even on a bad day, most of us parents know that we love our children. The question to ask ourselves, though, is whether we are showing them that love in a way that they can understand – in a way that really connects with them.

In his book *The 5 Love Languages® of Children*, psychologist Gary Chapman gives some insight into this. From years of counselling practice, he came up with a system to help people relate to one another better – the idea that there are five different ways of communicating love, which he calls the five 'love languages.' These are: words, time, actions, gifts and touch.[14]

For each of us, one or two of these languages will be the way that we feel most loved. The truth is, children need all five of these expressions of love, but as they get older we can begin

14 Gary Chapman, *The 5 Love Languages of Children*, Moody Press, 2012.

to work out which 'language' is most meaningful for them. We then have a powerful tool at our disposal. There is no greater gift we can give our children than for them to grow up knowing that they are loved.

In the next five chapters we are going to take a look at each of those 'love languages' in turn.

Speak words of life

♡ *love language 1*

♡

Much of the ancient book of Proverbs contains bite-sized wisdom about the way we use our words. One which I come back to time and again reads, 'The tongue has the power of life,'[15] reminding us of the sheer power of the words we speak.

In the early years, it is relatively easy to say encouraging and affirming words to our children. Our son learns to recognize the first letter of his name, or we catch our daughter sharing her toys, and we readily heap on praise and affirmation, telling them how clever, kind or generous they are. However, as time goes on, I have found it easy to slip into focussing on the negatives – nagging and pointing out what is wrong rather than spotting what is right and praising them for it.

I remember on one occasion when our youngest son asked if he could wash the car. He set to work with enthusiasm and made a reasonable job of it. However, armed with a hose and some free time he found lots of other things that he believed could do with dousing – including his brother. Everything within a mile radius was soaked, and I told him off in no uncertain terms for the mess he'd created. It was only later that I realized that I'd had nothing to say about the sparkling clean car – least of all making a point of praising him for it.

For one of our children, words of praise or encouragement are especially important. When he was about eleven years old,

15 Proverbs 18:21.

I was looking for something in his bedroom and discovered a shoebox under his bed. I took the lid off and found it was full of cards, notes and scraps of paper. They were all addressed to him and all included kind and encouraging words, which he had saved over the years. In the evening I asked him about it and he said, 'It's my treasure box. If I'm feeling sad I take it out and read them, and it makes me feel good.'

I remember meeting a stepdad at a Care for the Family event who told me about a special wall they had in their kitchen. They called it the 'sticker wall' because they stuck all kinds of things on it that they were proud of. He said the children weren't top of the class at school, nor were they great at sport. Nevertheless, all kinds of different achievements were celebrated – achievements that were special just for that family. And it wasn't just the children's achievements that were celebrated. One sticker read, 'You did really good driving today, Dad,' and another, 'Mummy is the best brownie-maker in the world.' When visitors came to the house, the children would grab them by the hand and drag them through to the kitchen to see the wall. He told me that he would watch their hearts swell with pride as visitors admired all the stickers.

There are so many different ways to give encouragement to our children. As well as recognizing successes and achievement, we can offer a word of praise to recognize character and effort. It was my grandson's first day at nursery, and he came running out clutching an enormous cardboard pink star with writing on it. My daughter looked to see what he had done to deserve the award – perhaps recognizing a letter or doing a lovely painting. But no – the star said, 'Ezra is kind and shared his tissues with the other children.' We laughed that sharing his snotty tissues in these Covid times was worthy of a mention in his first report.

But that nursery teacher was wise. Whether we are two or ninety-two, it feels good when someone praises our character.

And we can be creative in the way we deliver those encouraging words. 'You'll be great on the team today!' written on the banana in our child's lunch box, on the bathroom mirror, or a little note left on a pillow at night can all speak volumes.

Birthdays are also a great opportunity to speak kind and affirming words. One family we know has a tradition that after the candles have been blown out, they go round the table and each person says something that they love or admire about the birthday girl or boy that they can take with them into the year ahead. Words are not just for birthdays, but for life!

It's quality and *quantity time*

♡ *love language* 2

♡

For a number of years I believed the mantra that it is quality, not quantity time, that is important. But the sobering truth is that although we can't always give our children quantity time, they need both. So often it's the amount of time we spend with them that lays the foundation for our relationship and allows our quality time together to flourish. Author Gretchen Rubin said of our children's lives, 'The days are long, but the years are short,'[16] and now that our children have all flown the nest I know how true that is.

When he was little, our youngest, Henry, would jump into our bed every single morning, and soon a little ritual developed. As he snuggled in Richard would get up and have a shower, then throw his wet towel on top of Henry's head. He would laugh and giggle and pull it off.

This went on for years, morning after morning, but then one day as Richard got out of bed to have his shower we realized there was no Henry. He hadn't served notice on us that the game was over, and that he wasn't coming any more. But the fact was, that particular door on his childhood had now closed and no power on earth could open it. These times are precious.

With four children and busy lives, we found that we didn't often get one-to-one time when we could give them individual

16 Gretchen Rubin's one-minute video 'The Years are Short', *Gretchen Rubin*, 31 March 2014, gretchenrubin.com.

attention. And so we began a routine where one of us would take one of the children to Tesco's for breakfast on a Saturday morning. They would take it in turns and could decide which of us they wanted to go with them. All went well initially until I noticed that my husband increasingly became their companion of choice. Most of us are more insecure than we would like to admit and I began to wonder why they didn't want me to take them. Was I not a fun mummy? Further investigation revealed the truth. While breakfast with me involved cereal, orange juice and toast, I discovered that Richard was allowing them to enjoy chocolate eclairs and cheesy Wotsits, all washed down with a bottle of Coca-Cola! I decided to put their need for 'five a day' on hold just for one meal, as I reminded myself that the purpose of this outing never was about the breakfast. It was simply about spending time together, and I needed to relax the rules if I was ever going to get a look in.

Generally, the conversation wouldn't be about anything significant; it was just time spent together. We would talk about football stickers, glitter pens or the latest playground craze, but just occasionally we would hear about something more significant. I remember one of our children, who had recently started school, confiding to me in hushed tones across the table that he didn't want to go to the school the following week because he didn't know where to put his lunch box when he arrived. That one was fairly easily resolved. Others were more challenging. There were conversations about perceived injustices at school, struggles with friendships, or hopes and dreams that they had. Plans to play for Aston Villa, to be a fighter pilot, to own a mushroom restaurant called Fun-gi (… don't ask!) and to be a lead singer in a rock band were all dreamed up over breakfast at Tesco.

Making the most of the time we have with them – quality and quantity time – doesn't have to be complicated or expensive. It doesn't have to include deep conversation; it is time spent just *being* – hanging out or simply engaging in the ordinary things of family life together. Things like making biscuits, going to the park, watching a film or playing a game – activities where our children know that they, rather than the activity, are the focus of our attention.

Actions speak louder than words

♡ *love language* 3

♡

There are days as parents when it seems as if we have enrolled in long-term service. The list of jobs we do for our children can feel never-ending. When they are babies we feed them, wind them, soothe them, rock them to sleep, change nappies and begin the process over again. The tasks in the primary years may be more varied but are equally relentless. Cooking meals, tidying toys, washing clothes, finding socks, reading stories, making packed lunches, helping with homework, taking them to football, to Brownies, to karate … and on it goes. We certainly don't want to become doormats, and we do our children no favours if we don't equip them to do things for themselves, but for some children our actions are particularly important: they convey to them that we love them. As they get older we can focus on doing things for them that they can't do themselves, or, for whatever reason, perhaps haven't time to do for themselves.

Things I have done for my children that I know have meant a lot to them include helping them to find school books which they have mislaid, giving them a lift when they could have walked and making them a special packed lunch for a school trip. They are all jobs they could, and often did, do themselves, but just making the effort on those occasions to go the extra mile was a great way to say, 'I love you.'

GIFTS ARE NOT JUST FOR BIRTHDAYS

Gifts are not just for birthdays

♡ love language 4

♡

Our children are growing up in a consumer society where the overriding message is that they are what they own. As parents, we need to be wise in the way we use our money. While we cannot buy love, for some children gifts are tangible evidence of love and affection. And for those children it will be the thought behind the gift that conveys love and not the money involved.

When I first spent a night away as a speaker for Care for the Family, I bought some chocolate bars and put one on each of my children's beds. It became something of a tradition (though remembering to buy four Mars bars often felt like the last straw when trying to leave the house for a few days on the road). While all of our children enjoyed the chocolate, for one gifts are particularly important and it signified much more. It said, 'I love you. I loved you enough to think of buying this for you, and when you enjoy it, you will be reminded again that you are loved.'

Small gifts can make a difference – a tee-shirt when on holiday, a flower picked from the garden, a pencil or notebook, a rubber ball – all costing little in money but conveying love.

I was recently speaking at a summer conference and agreed to meet a young mother for coffee. Her daughter came over to join us. We hadn't met before, but she told me with much excitement that she had just celebrated her eighth birthday, and had come to ask for her birthday money to spend. The money was duly handed over with the warning that after it was spent it was gone. Two minutes later she came skipping back across the hall and with a broad grin on her face presented me with an enormous bar of Cadbury's chocolate. I was overwhelmed at her generosity. No amount of convincing could persuade her to take it back. Alongside words, gifts are one of the ways I most feel loved, and in eight-year-old Hannah I had found a kindred spirit. And that simple gesture had given a big clue to her parents that for Hannah, token gifts – not just on birthdays – would say to her 'I love you.'

PLEASE HOLD ME

♡ love language 5

An organization that I work with in South Africa has a wonderful programme that provides support and care for the hundreds of vulnerable children who have been orphaned as a result of HIV/Aids. The programme is called *Ngibambe*, which means 'please hold me.' I met Graeme Schnell, the CEO, when he visited the UK recently, and he told a moving story. Graeme had been visiting one of the Ngibambe projects. As he walked across the schoolyard, one of the children came running towards him, tripped and fell. Instinctively, he scooped her up in his arms to comfort her. Seconds later he found himself mobbed by a crowd of orphans, all clamouring to be picked up and held. These children were hungry for the profound power of touch to convey love.

Although it may feel awkward to start with, most parents don't need much teaching before they know how to cuddle a baby. And when our children are young we can take every opportunity to have a cuddle with them, to hold them – while watching the television, after they have taken a tumble, or when reading them a story or wrapping them in a soft, warm towel at bath time. For one of our children, this is his primary love language. If he ever had a cut knee, was upset or worried, just giving him a cuddle would reassure him. The world would seem safe and he would feel loved. He is now six foot three inches tall – and still occasionally enjoys a hug from his mother!

There are lots of opportunities to snuggle up with our children when they are young, but as they reach the end of the primary years it can begin to be less easy. Their need for a cuddle is no less great, but timing can be everything! One of our boys has never forgotten the moment that I gave him an enthusiastic hug at the school gate in full view of the first XV rugby team, who had just assembled on the coach. He still needed lots of hugs, but I learnt that they were best given before we left the house! A hand on the shoulder when they are at the computer, rough and tumble play, or sitting close to them while watching a film are all opportunities to show them we love them through the power of touch.

One thirteen-year-old boy put it like this: 'My parents don't hug me anymore. But when no one's looking, I wish they still would.'

Touch – it's simple, but so powerful. We all need a lot of *ngibambe*!

'Now's not really the time, Dad.'

DON'T LEAVE THEM TO THEIR OWN DEVICES

Don't leave them to their own devices

Eric Schmidt, the former chairman of Google, famously said: 'If you have a child, you'll notice that they have two states: asleep or online.'[17] It's a description parents may well recognize! And all the more so since the pandemic, when life became digital by default.

Digital technology now forms the backdrop of all our lives and is a wonderful resource, offering endless possibilities and inviting curiosity and learning. And it is an integral part of our children's world. In fact, before many of our children have learnt to read, they can navigate devices. I've been amazed as I've watched the skill of my pre-school grandchildren scrolling through photos on my phone; it seems second nature to them. But it is during the primary years that our children's use of technology changes dramatically. Using a parent's iPad to watch cartoons or favourite shows progresses before we know it to talking to family and friends online on their own smartphone or tablet. And the time they spend online changes, rising year on year from seven hours per week for children aged three to seven, to almost doubling to thirteen hours by the time they are eight. This increase in online interaction is something of a two-edged sword. With the increasing opportunity for exploration and learning, there is also an equal and opposite opportunity for exposure to risk and danger.

17 Patrick Kidd, 'Gaga, Jobs and Malala join ranks of quotable greats', *The Times*, 18 September 2014, thetimes.co.uk.

One of the main worries keeping many parents up at night is the sheer amount of time that their children spend glued to a glowing screen. And the pandemic has only exacerbated this concern, with website and app visits by children rising by 100%.[18]

For younger children, much of this time is spent on YouTube, which has overtaken television as their preferred viewing platform. Julie, parent to Ben, commented: 'Ben has his own iPad and spends hours on YouTube playing games and watching tricks and funny videos. He calls himself a YouTuber, and has his own channel. I know he gets a lot of enjoyment out of it, but I worry that it's taking over family life.'

But concerns about the amount of time our children spend online is only the tip of the iceberg. Other parental worries include the possibility of their children accessing inappropriate content or talking to strangers. There are reports of toddlers (known as TikTots) watching TikTok videos with all the dangers of livestreamed content.[19] One parent was dismayed to discover her child had been watching a Peppa Pig cartoon set in an inappropriate adult context. And as children get older, the insidious effect of social media and image-heavy platforms on their emotional wellbeing is added to the list of dangers. Increasingly, part and parcel of the online world includes sharing and connecting with friends in real time, bringing with it the possibility of online bullying and grooming.

Radio 4's *Today* programme recently featured an interview with Matteo who was in Year Five. Matteo plays a game online where one person has to draw something while the other person

18 Linda Geddes and Sarah Marsh, 'Concerns grow for children's health as screen times soar during Covid crisis', *The Guardian*, 22 January 2021, guardian.com.
19 'Rise of the five-year-old 'TikTots', *BBC News*, 29 March 2022, bbc.co.uk.

guesses what it is. 'They couldn't guess what I drew, and then someone called me an a-hole. I felt really upset so I straight away told my mum,' he told Victoria Derbyshire. Matteo's mother said she blocked that person but could do 'absolutely nothing' about it. 'I feel extremely guilty that he had access to that.'[20]

While we don't want to deny our children access to the online world, in the primary years they simply don't yet have the critical faculties to evaluate whether something is good or bad for them. Whether intentionally or by accident, their curiosity can put them in harm's way, so as parents, it is vital that we step up and take measures to keep them safe.

Minimum age guidelines for social networks are there to protect our children from harm. Each family will have their own approach as to how strictly they follow these guidelines, but it's worth remembering that apps and platforms that are not age-appropriate can expose children to things they may not be ready for. Viraj, who works in the IT industry and is a dad himself said: 'For us as a family, trying to keep to the PEGI ratings and age recommendations has made life so much easier. Our boys complain all the time and think we are much too strict compared to their friends' parents but we think it's important to hold the line. We also put all the necessary parental controls and filters in place, so at least when they are at home, they won't see anything that will upset them or that's not suitable for their age.' Maybe it should come as no surprise to find that Bill Gates, Steve Jobs and others working in Silicon Valley all had or have very strict guidelines on the use of technology in their homes.

20 'Online safety: Internet "not designed for children"', *BBC News*, 5 January 2017, bbc.co.uk.

While the issues may seem overwhelming, we certainly don't need to feel we're on the back foot! Schools will play their part in teaching children online safety, but that only goes so far. As their parents, we are the ones who really are best placed to help our children.

Here are some practical ideas to keep them safe in the digital world and help them embrace all its opportunities.

Put boundaries on screen time. When we crave some much-needed peace, being able to sit our child in front of a screen can be a lifesaver. But screens can also be overused. Having some age-appropriate family guidelines for time on screens is essential. Each family is different, and each child is different, so the most important thing is to develop a system that works for your family.

Talk to your children's friends' parents. Most parents attempting to set boundaries will be familiar with that infamous character 'Everyone Else's Parent'. 'Everyone Else's Parent' apparently not only lets their children have an Instagram account at primary school, but allows them to play on the Nintendo until 10pm every night of the week. Where possible, talk to other parents and try to agree the same ground rules for your children.

Set some screen-free times and places. Screens in the bedroom mean that many children simply aren't getting enough sleep. Encourage them to put their devices away an hour before bedtime and keep them out of the bedroom. Where possible, sit down together for meals and ban devices at the table.

Draw up a family media agreement. Sit down as a family and create an agreement about use of digital devices in the home that everyone (including parents!) signs up to. Make it fun – get some drinks and favourite snacks – and talk through the issues. The younger children are, the easier it is to put some ground rules in place.

Some good things to include:

- What devices can be used and when. At meal times? Late at night? Bedrooms or not?
- How much time can be spent on screens. Remember that not all screen time is the same. A game of Roblox is different from Maths homework, which is different again from a Zoom call with Granny.
- What platforms can be used and at what age.
- Ground rules for using digital technology on playdates and sleepovers.
- What information can or shouldn't be shared online.
- What your child should do if they are scared by something or made uncomfortable by something online.

The world is your oyster. As long as you remember to cover all the basics, you can customize the agreement in ways that will suit and meet the needs of your own family. Rather than making the agreement a list of don'ts, try to frame it as things that your children can do. And remember – it's not a straightjacket to restrict their freedom, but a seatbelt to keep them safe.

Use technology to enrich family life. Stay involved and be interested in your children's online world (even if Minecraft is not your activity of choice!). And encourage non-screen activities such as kicking a ball in the park, riding a scooter to the shops, or sitting down and playing an old-fashioned board game together.

Finally, something a little closer to home ... Be a good role model in the way you use technology. Remember that children take their cue from us, their parents. Before helping them develop a healthy relationship with technology, we may need to take stock of how we use it ourselves. If the first thing we do when we come in the door is to check our emails and if we are scrolling through Instagram when we pick them up from school, they will notice.

Our role as parents is a positive one, and in all this, our aim isn't to limit our children's freedom, but to teach them to manage that freedom well. There are practical things that we can and must do to keep them safe online during the primary years. But we can also use this time to teach them to make wise choices as they move into teenage and eventually adult life. We want to equip them to be able to enjoy and take advantage of all that the digital age has to offer.

LAUGHTER IS THE BEST MEDICINE

Laughter is the best medicine

It was a normal Wednesday afternoon when my friend Cathy embarked on the afternoon school run. A busy evening of back-to-back activities lay ahead. She pulled up outside the school and sat in the car with her daughter waiting for her sister to appear. Without guile, her daughter looked up and asked, 'Do you think you will be a better granny than you are a mummy?'

The question hit her broadside. I too have experienced moments like that – moments when our child's unwitting comments seem to suck all the air from our lungs.

Cathy asked what her daughter meant and listed all the many things she did for her. The CV was impressive: providing a taxi service, cooking meals, helping with music practice and homework, washing, ironing, braiding hair … and so it went on.

When she finished, her daughter nodded. 'I know,' she replied. 'It's just that we don't seem to have much fun.' Cathy later admitted to me that her daughter was right. Her family's busy schedule of activity meant there was little time for fun.

The primary years can be some of the busiest and most challenging. Younger children in the family may have gifted us with sleepless nights – add to that the physical exertion required to parent children in the daylight hours: walking them to school, driving them to football, swimming, helping with homework and refereeing disputes, and maybe it should be no surprise that sometimes a triple espresso or an energy drink is the only way we feel able to get through the day.

If we are working outside the home, this season often coincides with the very stage in our career when our work requires 110% of our focus and attention. For others, lack of a job leads to the intense pressure of seeking work and managing to make ends meet. Life can be hard. As well as all the ordinary things that are part of managing a home – kitchens to clean, meals to cook, clothes to iron, bills to pay – we may have other challenges; relationships under pressure, parenting alone, elderly parents to care for, illness or disability in the family, multiple births or children with additional needs. Somehow the relentlessness of life can take over and we go into survival mode.

The writer of the book of Proverbs wrote that 'A cheerful heart is good medicine'[21] and, 3,000 years later, science agrees. Laughter is good for us. Research shows that when we laugh, the tissue that lines our blood vessels expands. This increases blood flow and improves the health of our arteries.[22] Press the pause button on the treadmill of activity and take time to laugh together.

My husband is much better at this than me. I remember one 'sleepover' party (another misnomer!) for a number of ten-year-old boys. No sleep had taken place and it was now the small hours of the morning. Not only was I tired but I was imagining the wrath of Mrs Bishop descending on me the following morning when I returned her son Ned to her minus his obligatory eight hours sleep. My entreaties for the boys to quieten down had (unsurprisingly) fallen on deaf ears. Moreover Richard seemed to be ignoring the commotion and to add insult to injury had begun to snore. My exasperation boiled over and I woke him up and kicked him out of bed with a request to instil some discipline and some sleep to the occupants of George's bedroom.

21 Proverbs 17:22.
22 Lawrence Robinson, Melinda Smith, M.A. and Jeanne Segal, Ph.D. 'Laughter is the Best Medicine', *HelpGuide*, July 2021, helpguide.org.

He obligingly turned the light on and set off down the corridor. However instead of a descending calm, the noise level increased by 100 decibels plus. Armed with a giant Super Soaker water pistol he had crept into the room through a trap door from the roof space and begun the biggest water fight imaginable. The shouts and screams could be heard for miles! The boys may not have had their quota of sleep – and Mrs Bishop was as cross as I feared – but the boys enjoyed a party to remember.

Laughter can be about the smallest things – practical jokes, a plastic spider in the bed, funny stories at the meal table, hide and seek in the dark, watching favourite comedies on Netflix and even a water fight at 2am. Let's not take ourselves too seriously. Take time to laugh and have fun. Laughter really is the best medicine.

WE ALWAYS...

None of our family are gifted photographers, but a number of years ago we were given a video camera. In place of holiday snaps of children building sandcastles and playing cricket on the beach, we could capture footage of family life in real time. We now have a large drawer full of recordings and one of our favourite pastimes, particularly on birthdays or at Christmas, would be to get them out and re-live those memories. These evenings would be boring for any unsuspecting guests who might have the misfortune to be present for one of our family film nights. But to us, they were precious reminders of things we used to do when the children were little. They have captured the traditions and memories that make our family unique.

Each family has its own memories and traditions. If as adults we are asked to describe our childhood, more likely than not it won't be long before we alight on a family tradition. Many families have traditions around birthdays or Christmas that are simply the way that they do things – where they hang their decorations, their favourite recipes or the order of play for the day's events. We have a faded birthday banner that has ceremoniously been hung in our kitchen in February, March, April, May and twice in September for many years. Torn at the edges and stuck together with Sellotape, it has seen better days. I recently decided it had had its day and should be replaced with a new one. To my surprise my suggestion was met with outrage from our children. Apparently this bedraggled banner, plays a vital role in celebrating birthdays in our household. Birthdays just wouldn't be birthdays without it because 'we always' put it up. Suffice to say, the banner remains.

Some family traditions simply emerge of their own accord while others are created deliberately, but they all put precious deposits in our family memory bank. Our family traditions over the years have included everyone piling into our bed at 7am on birthdays, buns after school on Fridays, pizza on family nights, spending October half-term with the same two families, having breakfast at Tesco, singing all five verses of 'Auld Lang Syne' raucously at midnight on New Year's Eve, camping in the Quantocks, wearing silly hats to the cinema and playing charades on Christmas Day, to name just a few. Think about what traditions you already have, and maybe even create some more. If you can't think of any, your children will help you!

Traditions and shared memories are important for children as they help build a sense of family identity and belonging – what one academic called 'a sense of connectedness.' If we are in a blended family, then we may need to combine different ways of doing things – perhaps keeping some traditions and making new ones together – but as we do that we will find we are putting down roots and building a new identity. We are creating a 'We always … ' memory for our children's future.

Lay the table

In recent years, fewer families are making time to sit around a table and eat together. Busy, conflicting schedules have meant that meals on the go or in front of screens have increasingly become the norm.

When our children were younger, we tried to make family mealtimes a priority. They were far from perfect. Children would wriggle off their chairs, poke each other, and refuse to eat what was on their plate. Drinks would be upset and boys would be daft with the tomato ketchup (which they argued could be included as one of their 'five a day'). Despite the mayhem, I am so glad that we persevered with having meals together as looking back, some of our best family times took place around the table.

I met Jenny, a single parent, at a Care for the Family event. She said this about the importance of eating together as a family:

> I have three children aged between four and ten. I work full time outside the home and life is hectic. Often the meals we eat during the week are on the run, but on Friday evenings and Sunday lunchtimes we eat 'properly' as a family.
>
> I've tried hard to make these meals special occasions. Each child has a task – helping with the cooking, laying the table, washing up – and although persuading the middle one to do anything at all is a battle every time, we usually get there eventually. On Fridays the meal could still be something ordinary like beans

on toast, but we sit at a laid table and we talk. The telly's off. No screens at the table.

I try not to have a go at the children during these meals – I want them to be enjoyable … Of course, getting a conversation going is sometimes like dragging teeth out – especially with the eldest one; but we've had some brilliant – and enlightening – times.

The other night, I got home early on a Tuesday and they'd laid the table for a 'proper' meal. One of them said, 'I know it's not the right night, Mum, but can we do it anyway?' I thought, 'Yes!'[23]

We recently looked after our two-year-old granddaughter for the weekend while her parents were at a wedding. Her routine (that I have been keen to encourage when I am in charge!) would be to give her an early lunch and then a sleep. On this occasion we were running late and I decided to stretch the ground rules and keep her up for Sunday lunch together, and give her a sleep afterwards.

It had been an action-packed weekend, and I was looking forward to hearing her tell her parents all about it, when they came to collect her. To my surprise, at top of her list was that we had had lunch 'all togever'. Even at two, there had been something memorable about sitting down together as an extended family that went far beyond enjoying the food that was served.

---

23 Rob Parsons, *The Sixty Minute Family*, Lion Books, 2010, pp27–28.

Research shows that eating together, even once a week, offers a number of benefits. It's a great opportunity for conversation – to discover what is going on in our children's lives, what they are thinking and hoping for. With our own children a simple game called 'High/Low' helped with that. It simply involved taking it in turns to say what our 'high' and our 'low' had been for that particular day. The children were not always cooperative, but just sometimes we heard about a falling out in the playground or an achievement on the sports field that otherwise they might not have told us about.

Mealtimes give children the chance to grow social skills and develop language, but most importantly they encourage a sense of identity and belonging.[24]

In practical terms, having meals round the table together can be difficult to organize. But remember that the menu doesn't need to rival *MasterChef*. Keep it simple, and give the children a sense of ownership by involving them in planning what to eat, laying the table, and the cooking itself, as far as appropriate for their age. Even a four-year-old can choose a topping and put it on a pizza.

And for many families different schedules shifts and commitments mean that meals need to be in more than one sitting. When we were at this stage of family life a tip I picked up from a friend was once the children's food was on the table, instead of getting on with the jobs that were pressing – washing up, tidying or catching up on emails – she would intentionally make a pot of tea for herself, sit down with the children and enjoy the time together.

It may not always be possible but if we can, laying the table even once a week will build that sense of connection in our family life.

24 E. Cook, R. Dunifon, 'Parenting in Context, Do Family Meals Really Make a Difference?', *Cornell University*, 2012, human.cornell.edu.

LET THEM PLAY

The opening paragraph of our daughter's first school report made for entertaining reading: 'Charlotte likes to begin the day by dressing up. Her costume of choice generally includes a pink tutu, a Viking helmet, and a feather boa.' Knowing her sense of fashion at the time, I had to smile, but I also remember thinking I would have preferred a progress report on her aptitude for reading, writing and arithmetic – the things that I considered to be the 'real' business of education.

Mrs McDonell, her teacher, no doubt had a twinkle in her eye as she penned that report. She was a wonderful teacher – colourful, expressive, warm and generous – a true creative. She loved to encourage the children to use all their senses, to imagine, to create and to play. Each of our children grew to love Mrs McD – she opened up the wonder of creation and the infinite world of the imagination, and taught them the value of an enquiring mind.

Jean Piaget, the Swiss psychologist, was particularly interested in the role of play in child development. He famously said, 'Play is the work of children' and demonstrated that play can be an effective vehicle for children to learn about their world.[25]

25 Jean Piaget, *Play, Dreams and Imitation in Childhood*, Heinemann, 1945.

There are a myriad of ways that children play. Building and demolishing sand castles, dressing up as pirates or princesses, pretend games of schools, shops, hospitals, happy families, games with dolls, cars, teddies, Lego, board games or computer games – all of these provide fun and enjoyment in themselves. But in addition, each aspect of play provides a relaxed atmosphere where all kinds of learning can occur and an opportunity for social skills to develop. As parents, we would do well to learn from Mrs McD not to have every minute of our child's day programmed for 'learning', but to make time for play, creativity and imagination. We might not feel that we ourselves are the creative type – or even if we were, by the time we became adults the world had knocked it out of us – but we can allow our children to lead the way.

My friend Nicky's children are a techie household – they have every game, gadget and gizmo going. A 110-inch screen to rival the local cinema stretches across the living room wall; gaming consoles, iPads and iPhones litter the floor. However, when I visited recently, they were ignoring the contents of the Apple store and were engaged in a game of make-believe. They were marooned on a desert island with Robinson Crusoe and had dragged duvets downstairs to make a raft so they could escape. They set about piling tins of beans and tuna onto the raft so they would have provisions for their time at sea.

My friend, seemingly oblivious to the resulting disarray in her kitchen cupboard, offered to swim to the shore to find the life jackets. Halfway across the 'ocean', she looked up and explained that this was their favourite game. And watching them play, I saw she was right. I reflected that in later life these children will remember this scene. The expensive skateboards, bikes and electronic gadgets may be fun, but nothing beats an adventure on a raft with a tin of tuna, a tin of beans and Man Friday for company.

It has been said that the best gift a child can receive is the simple gift of play and imagination. As parents, we may want to buy our children expensive toys, sometimes because we didn't have them ourselves when we were young. But we can be so busy giving our children what we didn't have that we don't have time to give them what we did have. And that includes the simple gift of play and imagination.

Sometimes 'playing safe' is dangerous

As a young boy growing up on the Isle of Wight, adventurer Bear Grylls was taught by his father to climb, to sail and, most importantly, to dream. His bedroom was covered in posters of Mount Everest. One day, Bear vowed to climb Everest – a dream he and his father nurtured together. His father knew the risks. Every year, the death toll on the mountain rises, and for every ten mountaineers who make it to the top, one will die. Despite the risks, however, his parents encouraged Bear's spirit of adventure, and at 7.22am on 26th May 1998, aged just twenty-three, he entered *The Guinness Book of Records* as one of the youngest climbers to reach the summit of the world's highest mountain.

Bear has since become the youngest ever Chief Scout, and around the world he is one of the most recognized faces associated with survival and outdoor adventure.

While our children may not be about to join an expedition to the Himalayas, we would do well as parents to foster in them the ability to dream and to have that same spirit of adventure.

Pick up any children's storybook, popular film or game and you are likely to discover characters involved in exciting escapades. Whether it is a gallant prince rescuing a beautiful princess from the castle, a young boy fighting a giant and winning against all the odds, a spine-tingling spy thriller or an adventure with aliens in space, we celebrate adventure. By temperament, some children will be more risk-averse than others, but at heart, most delight in the thrill of adventure and new discovery. As parents, our every instinct is often to keep our children safe. But if we allow that to govern our approach to parenting, always saying 'No' to any exploit that has any element of risk attached, we will be denying them the chance to develop some essential life skills.

The truth is that real adventure generally involves stepping outside the front door, away from the comfort of the living room. Find opportunities for them to have an adventure and learn new skills. It might be an organized camp or weekend away, or simply a night sleeping in a tent. It might be climbing a pole, building a fire and toasting marshmallows, constructing a den, jumping off a rock or learning to ride a bike, to skateboard or to surf. Whatever it is, the exhilaration of pushing the boundaries to master new things harnesses children's natural curiosity and gives them an opportunity to be creative and develops confidence and wellbeing.

Wrapping them in cotton wool may mean no tumbles, plasters or trips to A&E, but unless we encourage risk-taking appropriate to their age, we will be denying our children the opportunity to build the character and resourcefulness that will enable them to dream … and then to conquer their own mountains in life.

BOUNDARIES GIVE SECURITY

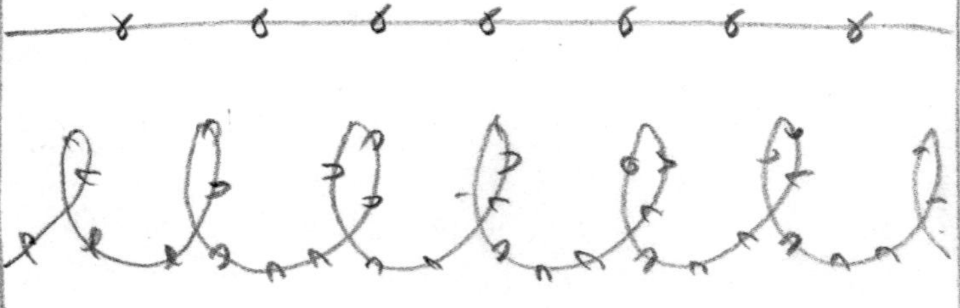

Boundaries give security

It was Daniel's first day at school. He had been up since 5.30am and could hardly contain his excitement. By 8.30am the rest of the family were finally dressed and ready to go, the baby strapped into the buggy. Clutching his new shiny blue lunch box, Daniel hurtled out of the front door and down the path to the gate. His mother shouted at him to wait, but her entreaty fell on deaf ears. Pushing the buggy at speed, she set off down the road and tried to catch him up but to no avail – he was round the corner and out of sight in seconds. As she reached the corner she called urgently to him to wait for her at the crossing. Oblivious, he turned left and continued to sprint towards the main road where she knew that two lanes of commuter traffic would take no prisoners. Fortunately for Daniel he was not the only child walking to school that day, and his mother turned the corner in time to see him enveloped by a guardian angel wearing a bright yellow high-visibility jacket, and carrying a large lollipop. After school, Daniel's parents sat him down for 'a big talk', after which he was left in no doubt about the importance of boundaries and the consequences if they were crossed.

Children need boundaries, not just for road safety but for life. And it is our job to put the boundaries in place – we are their parents, not their best friend.[26]

Our children's job, of course, is to push against those boundaries – that is the equation! Boundaries are not so much

26 Patricia Kerig, *Implications of Parent-Child Boundary Dissolution for Development Psychopathology: 'Who is the Parent and Who is the Child?*, The Haworth Press, 2005.

about discipline as about safety, and in setting boundaries in line with our family values, we are giving them a gift: we will be building in them a deep sense of security that will last a lifetime.

CHOOSE YOUR STYLE

The approach parents take to setting and maintaining boundaries for their children can take different forms. At one end of the spectrum is what experts call the 'authoritarian' style of parenting. Authoritarian parents can be perfectionists at heart: they like to be in control. In this home there are lots of rules and each one is enforced regardless of circumstances.

Homework has to be done before any screen time is allowed, meals are at set times and children are expected to sit still and finish all the cauliflower on their plate. There may well be a rota on the fridge door for jobs to be done around the house, and this is adhered to with military precision. I remember one of our children stopped wanting to go to a friend's house because there were so many rules – I think he was scared of putting a foot wrong!

This sheep and pen here represents the authoritarian style of parenting. The good news is that there is clarity. The children know exactly where the line is drawn – they know what is and isn't allowed. However, there's a flip side to the coin. The problem with this style of parenting is that the child can feel hemmed in and controlled with little room for creativity or independence.

Right at the other end of the spectrum is the 'permissive' style of parenting. Children with permissive parents are often the envy of other children, particularly those who come from homes where authoritarian parenting is the style of choice. Their parents are chilled and relaxed, there are few boundaries and if they are crossed there are no consequences. The children decide whether or not to do their homework and there are no limits on screen time. Meal times are whenever people are hungry and there's no requirement for the children to sit still, eat cauliflower or in fact to do anything they don't want to do that day. Jobs are done by whoever is around at the time, and family life is chaotic but carefree. The mantra of these parents is: 'Do what you like.'

This second sheep illustrates the permissive style of parenting. The good news is that the child has complete freedom to explore and discover things for themselves. There is plenty of room for creativity. However, without boundaries our children can feel lost. They need boundaries, if only to push against.

The style of parenting to aim for is the 'assertive' style. Assertive parents know the importance of setting boundaries, but set as few rules as possible in line with the things they believe are important. The rules that they do set are enforced. For example, they may set ground rules about homework, but they are prepared to agree exceptions when a reasonable request is made. They monitor their children's screen time and negotiate it with them. There is a routine for family meals – children are expected to sit at the table and to try to eat everything, but the parents will compromise over some things (usually cauliflower). As a general rule, family members are expected to help clear the table, but this can be relaxed on occasions. They give their children a clear understanding of what they expect, give explanations and listen to opposing views. This style of parenting is sometimes described as 'firm but fair'.

The third picture illustrates the assertive style of parenting. Children can see where the boundaries are and so feel safe, accepted and loved. They have room to explore, to grow in independence and to push against the boundaries in the knowledge that they are there for their benefit.

Our approach to parenting will be influenced by the way we have been parented ourselves, as well as by our individual temperament and personality. With the benefit of hindsight, most of us will look back and regret having either laid down the law too firmly or been too relaxed on a specific issue. None of us will get this right all of the time. It has been well said that 'rules without relationship lead to rebellion'. If we can aim for the assertive parenting style – to be firm and fair in the context of relationship with our children – we will be giving them a secure base from which to explore the world.

And just a word on these issues to those parenting children with additional needs. Parents of children with additional needs face a whole set of unique challenges and experiences which can place extra demands on the family. These children have the same need for boundaries. They will feel loved, safe and secure when they know what is expected of them. As a parent, try to have realistic expectations of your child's behaviour – not too high (but not too low either!).

Nicola Watson, co-ordinator of Care for the Family's Additional Needs Support service, reflected on challenges faced by parents in this area:

'We become the expert on our own children. What works one day may not work – or even be appropriate – on another. Boundaries are perhaps more flexible depending on the needs of the child and the way that they are applied may vary too. Onlookers may think we're being too lenient or indeed too rigid. It's not unusual to feel judged when what we need is compassion and understanding. Managing behaviour well is challenging without the added 'extras' that children with additional needs bring.'

A significant challenge in setting boundaries with children with additional needs can be communication – you may feel you are having to say the same thing time and again. Bucketloads of patience and understanding is required, as well as the ability to reassess what is really important and to let some things go.

CHOOSE YOUR BATTLES

Choose your battles

As someone who can veer towards the authoritarian style of parenting, one of the most helpful pieces of wisdom I received was, 'Choose your battles.'

There are so many battles we can have: 'Tidy your bedroom', 'Eat your crusts', 'Keep the water in the bath', 'Wear your coat to school', 'Put your toys away', 'Come to the table', 'Keep out of the puddles', 'Brush your hair', 'Clean your teeth', 'Learn your spellings', 'Hang up your bag', 'Don't pinch your sister'. The list is endless. If we make every issue a battle to fight, not only will we wear ourselves out but, our children will never learn which things are really important.

As a family, we spent a memorable October half-term staying with friends in a beautiful harbour-side cottage in Cornwall. We planned to mark the final evening by going out for a meal together. The restaurant was across the estuary, and so instead of driving round by car we decided to add to the fun of the evening by piling into their small inflatable dinghy. We agreed to meet on the jetty at 6.30pm.

The autumn air meant that by then it was quite chilly. We had dressed up for the occasion and, undeterred, put on an extra layer and went down to the jetty.

Everyone, that is, except our third son, Ed, who was then six. He had a new full-length wetsuit, and his six-year-old logic was that if we were going in a boat, a wetsuit was the correct thing to wear. In contrast, my adult reasoning told me that everyone else had dressed up for a meal out and wetsuits were for the beach. Despite my best efforts, Ed refused to be persuaded to change. At 6.45pm, with the rest of the party getting colder by the minute waiting for our arrival, I paused and asked myself the question: is this a battle I need to fight? And so down we went to the jetty and over to the restaurant, Ed in a wetsuit and everyone else dressed for an evening out.

It was a hilarious evening that we still remember. Ed did overheat, and getting in and out of the wetsuit when he visited the loo caused a queue that rivalled the Boxing Day sales. But looking back, we nearly missed not only on the fun of the evening, but also the memory we would carry with us for years to come by my choosing to have a battle that wasn't really worth fighting.

Correct clothing for a meal out may be a battle you want to fight. If it is, stay firm and fight it tooth and nail. But be careful, because you will almost certainly have far more important battles to fight further down the road. Decide what things are important to you, then say 'Yes' to as many of your children's requests as possible, and 'No' to the rest.

Choose your battles.

SAY WHAT YOU MEAN AND MEAN WHAT YOU SAY

Say what you mean and mean what you say

If we set a clear boundary and our children either sneak across it quietly or march defiantly over it, it is vital that there are consequences. If we simply turn a blind eye, our children will soon come to believe that we don't say what we mean or mean what we say.

I remember learning that lesson from another parent. Our eldest child, George, had been to play at a friend's house and in their living room were two enormous beanbags, full of polystyrene balls. A recent visit to see Father Christmas had evidently kicked the two boys' creativity into overdrive and inspired them to invent a wonderful game. They had opened the beanbag, tipped out all the polystyrene balls and made what they called a 'Winter Wonderland'.

Under the misguided belief that they were happily occupied playing Lego, my friend had enjoyed a moment of peace and quiet, and when she put her head round the door later was ill-prepared for the re-landscaping of her living room that had occurred. Kirsty Allsop would have been proud. Several hours later the Hoover had made few inroads into the scene of devastation, as the polystyrene balls gained a static electricity of their own. She was not impressed! She let the boys know in no uncertain terms that this game was never to happen again and, in fact, if it was repeated, George would be sent straight home.

A fortnight later, the boys decided to take a chance. They opened the beanbags again and a second snow scene was created that was even more splendid than the first. But this mother had set a boundary and had spelled out the consequence of crossing it. Before the boys could blink, she terminated the game and returned a shocked and sheepish-looking George to our doorstep. That day those boys learnt that when that parent said something, she meant it. Although there were many more moments of creative play involving duvets, towels, chairs and the contents of the food cupboard, they never did open up the beanbags again.

We were at a neighbour's birthday party. Anna had been invited along with her children, a six-year-old girl and twin four-year-old boys. The party overflowed into the garden, and as the afternoon drew in we gathered around the fire pit. As we chatted, Anna's twins came running towards the fire. She caught them by the hand, bent down to their level, looked them in the eye and put on a very solemn voice. She showed them a line on the paving stone on the ground and explained to them they could go up to that line, but not an inch further. If anyone went over the line, they would have to leave the party. Two little red heads nodded in agreement. One twin stayed firmly where he was, but the other looked her straight the eye and deliberately put the toe of his trainer a centimetre over the mark. That little boy was saying to his mother, 'I wonder how much you really mean what you say?' And he discovered she did. For that four-year-old, the party ended early that day.

As a parent I got into a rut with one particular child, and meted out the same consequence for every misdemeanour. His favourite Newcastle football shirt would be confiscated and stowed away on top of the kitchen cupboard for whatever length of time fitted the crime. Apart from the fact that this tee-shirt spent much of its life out of circulation, it occurred to me rather late in the day that apart from being an inconvenience, this consequence didn't teach a lesson. It is generally better to see if we can find a consequence that is in some way linked to the offence, which is what happens in life. If I fail to put the rubbish out for collection, the City Council won't confiscate my favourite 'tee-shirt, but I will have to live with the smell of rubbish and the possibility of rats. It's not always possible but examples might be, 'You didn't tidy the toys when I asked you to, Mummy had to do it and so there will only be time for one story tonight not two.' Or, 'When I asked you to come for tea you carried on gaming, so there will be no more screens this evening.'

We had been speaking at a parenting event on the issue of setting and maintaining boundaries when a parent shared her experience of the challenge of getting this right. Her daughter had been misbehaving, and she found herself saying, 'If you do that one more time then we won't be going to *The Lion King*.' Her daughter did it again. That parent then had a problem. They had already bought tickets for *The Lion King*, they were going with another family, and they were booked on a coach to London. As they arrived at the theatre and her daughter made her way down the aisle with a large bag of sweets in one hand and a bucket of popcorn in the other, she realized that it had not been the most effective consequence she could have come up with.

Say what you mean and mean what you say – and just make sure you can really follow through on those consequences.

REMEMBER THE THREE DS

Sitting round a campfire on a weekend away, we struck up a conversation with a family friend who was now a grandfather. He and his family had been through some challenging times and, as the night drew in, he shared with us some of the lessons learnt along the way. In talking about boundaries and discipline, he told us about a framework that had been helpful to them. He called it 'the principle of the three Ds' and soon after that we adopted it into our family life.

He explained to us that there were three behaviours all beginning with the letter 'D' that were out of bounds for their family. They were:

Dishonesty   *Disrespect*   *Disobedience*

He described the three Ds as being like three sides of a triangle. His children were free to do anything they liked within the triangle, but must not cross those three thresholds. The three things were based on the things they believed were important to them as a family:

Honesty – there would be consequences for telling lies or other dishonesty. For example, claiming to have cleaned your teeth when the toothbrush was still bone dry, or denying you had eaten the chocolates from your brother's Advent calendar when a stash of wrappers had been discovered under your bed. A failure to own up would always be treated more seriously than the original misdemeanour.

Respect – for other people and their belongings. There were consequences for rudeness, thoughtlessness and disrespect. For example, refusing to thank Mrs Jones for tea or for giving your sister's doll a tattoo with a permanent pen.

Obedience – there were consequences for deliberately being disobedient. For example, throwing a cricket ball in the kitchen (in the knowledge that it was for garden use only) or refusing to turn off the screen and come to the meal table when asked.

Different families will have different things they believe are important, so decide what things are important to you. Once you have done this, find a way of communicating them to your children so that they know where they stand. We found over the years that although the three Ds was a simple formula, it covered almost every eventuality, and when it came to setting boundaries, it wasn't a bad place to start.

'ok. I've created a simple set of principles we're all going to live by. I call it the 4 As, the 6 Bs, 7 Cs 2 Ds, 8 Es ...'
?

CHILDISH IRRESPONSIBILITY
OR
DISOBEDIENCE?

Childish irresponsibility or disobedience?

If your child has crossed a boundary, before reacting it can be helpful to press the pause button and ask yourself, 'Are they simply acting their age?' In other words, are they old enough to have understood the boundary and the consequence, or does their action simply reflect their immaturity? Is this a childish act for which they are not responsible or are they actually being disobedient?

Our family had been invited to a wedding, and to avoid an early start we had arranged to stay with friends the night before. Breakfast the next morning was accompanied with shouts of joy and delight from our boys as their eyes alighted on a giant box of Coco Pops. Chocolate cereal in our house was a special treat reserved for high days and holidays, and they couldn't believe their good fortune! In the excitement, little hands weren't big enough to grasp the packet, and chocolate cereal and milk spilt everywhere, including all down the wedding shirts that, in a misguided triumph of hope over experience, I had suggested they wore for breakfast.

Frustrating and annoying as it was, I only had myself to blame. They were excited and the disaster was the result of childish high spirits rather than disobedience or naughtiness – they couldn't be expected to know that they couldn't hold the packet.

A few months later, Coco Pops featured again. On the Monday morning I made a trip to Sainsbury's to buy a packet for a birthday breakfast the following Wednesday. The whole family knew that the Coco Pops were for the birthday breakfast and not for general consumption. So on Tuesday morning when I discovered that not only had the cereal been opened and eaten, but (adding insult to injury) the free toy dinosaur inside had been taken from the packet, my reaction was very different to the one I had on the day of the wedding. One of our children had been deliberately disobedient. They knew what they were doing and they knew there would be consequences.

In the heat of the moment it can be easy to overreact, but just pausing for a moment to consider whether our children are being deliberately naughty or simply acting their age can mean that we respond appropriately to their actions.

LABEL THE ACTION, NEVER THE CHILD

The children's playground rhyme, 'Sticks and stones may break my bones but words will never hurt me,' is simply not true. Most of us can remember only too well hurtful words that have been spoken to us. When our children are testing us to the limit, it can be so easy to slip into saying things that not only convey our frustration or anger at what they have done, but also label their character.

I came across the following letter which underlines the importance of the way we speak to our children:

My father left our family home when I was young and we lost touch with him. I will never know if he ever tried to get in touch, but if he did, my mother kept it from us. When I was just ten, my mother died suddenly and unexpectedly. I was sent to live with my great-aunt. I can understand it, as the last thing she needed was a ten-year-old to look after, but she never made me feel welcome. She told me repeatedly that I was a nuisance and in the way. Looking back, the impact of her words has shaped who I am. As an adult I have low self-esteem and little confidence. I am working to change that, but I believe my life could have been so different if, in those early years, those who cared for me had pointed out what was right with me rather than what was wrong.

My daughter recalls a time at junior school when she was given the chance to try a number of new activities – Brownies, swimming, gymnastics, recorder and drama club, to name just a few.

She embraced these opportunities wholeheartedly – only to want to give each up after the first term. Reflecting on this pattern of behaviour and thinking I could nip it in the bud, I said to her, 'Don't be a quitter; persevere. Don't keep giving up!' But what I had thought was a call to arms and an exhortation to aim high, she saw as a rebuke. It was years later that she told me that the words that she heard me say were, 'You *are* a quitter.' The power of those words shaped how she saw herself, and it took her several years to believe otherwise.

I know that in the heat of the moment I have sometimes used words carelessly to my children. Rather than commenting on them – 'You *are* so selfish/unkind/naughty … (fill in the blank)' – we would do well instead to describe their behaviour. Rather than saying, 'You are unkind to leaving Zola out of your game' we might say, 'When you wouldn't let Zola join in, that was an unkind thing to do.' Describing behaviour leaves open the possibility of change.

We all wear labels from our past; some are easier to read than others. As parents, we have an important role in shaping our children's character and bringing correction when it is needed. But as we do that, let's ensure that, above all, what they hear loudly and clearly are positive words that will form their identity and build their character for years to come.

CONSEQUENCES ARE THE BEST TEACHERS

As our children moved on from primary school, a regular message would wing its way to my phone. The text would ask (very politely) whether, if I was not doing anything, could I 'pop over' (aka drive across town in rush hour traffic) with forgotten football boots/guitar music/maths homework/permission slip/bus fare/inhalers … fill in the blank.

Provided I was in town my response depended on the age of the child, and their form in this area, as well the consequences of not having the item in question (the inhaler was delivered pronto!). As parents, our natural instinct is to make life as easy as possible for our children – we don't like seeing them suffer the consequences of mistakes – but sometimes in life, lessons are best learnt the hard way.

'The helicopter parent'[27] is a term used to describe the overprotective parent – the parent who hovers overhead, paying close attention to their child's every need and swoops in at every turn, rotor blades whirring to prevent catastrophe. Forgotten sports kit or other items are delivered immediately, excuses are provided for a failure to do music practice, and homework is

27 E. Lee, J. Bristow, C. Faircloth and J. Macvarish, *Parenting Culture Studies*, Palgrave Macmillan, 2014.

done by proxy. Helicopter parents operate from the very best of intentions, wanting to protect their offspring from the knocks of life, but the results often put their children at a disadvantage.

Resilience is the ability to handle the everyday frustrations, challenges and disappointments that life throws at us and to bounce back from them. Our children are born with the capacity to learn resilience, and as parents we are best placed to help build and develop this quality in their lives. Having the resolve to sometimes let our children learn the hard way has the power to unleash resourcefulness, resilience and creativity in

them – qualities which will stand them in good stead in years to come.

Where there is a will, there is usually a way!

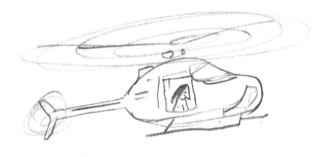

SHOULDER

TO

SHOULDER

Shoulder to shoulder

Growing up, I enjoyed a television series called *Shoulder to Shoulder*. It told the story of Emmeline Pankhurst and her fellow suffragettes as they campaigned at the turn of the twentieth century for the right for women to vote. One of the reasons they were able to make an impact was their singular unity of purpose.

'Shoulder to shoulder' is not a bad mantra for couples parenting together. We need to have that same determination to stand united. If one parent is seen as a soft touch, or if there is a chink of light between you, most single-minded youngsters will be able to use it to their advantage. Even if we disagree with a line taken by the other parent, a show of unity is vital.

Annika asked ten-year-old Nathan to turn off his game and come and help with the washing up. Despite repeated nagging, he refused to come, until finally Annika snapped. She dispatched him to his bedroom, confiscating his games console until the morning. A few minutes later his dad arrived home. He had been looking forward to seeing the children before bedtime. Annika told him what happened and he went upstairs to find Nathan. Ten minutes later she heard shouts of delight and poked her head around the door, only to see father and son engaged in a game of FIFA on the confiscated games console. Suffice it to say the conversation that followed is probably best left to the imagination!

There have been occasions when, in the heat of the moment, either Richard or I have meted out a draconian punishment that does not fit the crime. At those times it has been a challenge for the other one of us not to commiserate with our child at the unfairness of the situation, rather than simply discussing it afterwards.

If we are living apart and co-parenting, it is an extra challenge, but seeking to be of one mind as parents is vital. And if we are bringing up our children alone, it can feel exhausting to be the one who continually has to set and maintain boundaries. In this situation find friends who can help and support you – a community that can encourage you in this most important of roles.

ENJOY THE GENERATION GAME

Wednesday afternoons were a special day for our elder two children. When they were at primary school we were fortunate to have their grandparents living nearby, and it was the day the children would visit them for tea. Their grandfather would meet them at the school gate and then walk them home via the bakery, where they would spend hours choosing two small cakes. After rehearsing all the options at length (my father is a very patient man!), they would almost always make the same choices: a pink cake with a strawberry on the top for Charlotte and anything large with chocolate and quantities of cream for George. The cakes would be ceremoniously placed into a box and taken to their grandparents' house where they would be readily consumed.

The children would spend the next hour being read stories, doing jigsaw puzzles and playing Snakes and Ladders or Checkers, games that never seemed to lose their appeal. They look back on those afternoons with great fondness, not least because of the foundation that was laid for their relationship with their grandparents.

I wonder what images are conjured up in your mind as you consider the word 'grandparent'. It could be a bespectacled old lady wiping the flour from her hands as she puts the finishing touches to a Victoria sponge, a lady in a bed with rather large teeth talking to a small girl in red, or perhaps somebody more fearsome altogether. But whatever view we may have, the truth is that grandparents are varied in the extreme. There are grandmothers who have thousands of followers on TikTok and post daily, there are skydiving granddads, career-ladder-climbing Nannies, Bampas, Poppas or whatever other tags get attached to the older members of our families. And there are at least five million valiant grandparents providing childcare and enabling grateful parents to return to work.

But just as grandparents differ from one another in their lifestyles, there are differences emotionally. Some people cannot wait until they become grandparents – and adopt the title and the role as though they are born to it. Others are not at all sure they are ready (or old enough!) for this task and actually a little nervous as to whether they will measure up.

But at their best, there is no doubt that grandparents can have wonderful influence on the lives of their grandchildren. As parents, even if family relationships are complicated, it is worth making the effort to give the opportunity to enable that to happen. One eight-year-old put it like this, 'Everybody should have a grandmother, because they're the only grown-ups that have time.' One academic called the relationship between grandparents and grandchildren 'an emotionally uncomplicated form of love.' If that is true, then it has to do with the fact that generally they do not bear ultimate responsibility for the child. In other words, they can enjoy their grandchildren's good traits without feeling guilty about the bad ones. And perhaps it is that very lack of ultimate responsibility that can allow grandparents to truly give the gift of unconditional love. They are not trying to get all that homework in on time, the recorder practice done, or having to demand that the hamster is at least found, if not fed. One child said, 'Being with my gran is like having a bath that is full of bubbles and with no cold bits.'

But perhaps, above all, grandparents can help a child answer some of the deepest questions: 'Who am I?' 'Do I belong?' and 'What is my place in the world?'. So much of that has to do with discovering roots – and grandparents are wonderful for that. A Malian writer famously said, 'In Africa when an old man dies, it's a library burning.'[28] But the library shouldn't burn. I didn't know my grandparents, and watching my children now and their relationship with their grandparents I see now just what I missed out on growing up. If your parents are alive, encourage them to tell the stories of when they were children, share old photographs and if possible take your children to places that were important to them – their school, their home, their workplace. A beautiful quote popularly attributed to author and columnist Lois Wyse says, 'Grandparents connect the dots from generation to generation.'

But before we get too starry-eyed, let's be honest enough to admit that there can be problems with grandparents – and generally in two areas: too near and too far away. We all know stories of rogue grandparents who interfere, criticize or, as in one spectacular piece of misjudgement we came across, announce, 'Great news, I've just agreed to buy the other half of your semi! I wanted to surprise you.' I think it's fair to say that she achieved that, although her son and daughter-in-law had the last laugh when three months later they agreed to buy the other half of somebody else's!

28 Amadou Hampâté Bâ, quoted in Kokouvi Ketika, 'Aspects of African Civilization: Person, Culture, Religion', 1972, academia.edu.

'Too near' needn't just be a geographical thing – more that grandparents can be simply interfering. And perhaps here above all we need the wisdom of Solomon. On the one hand perhaps we can afford to be understanding and realize that they have all this hard-won experience of raising children but, frustratingly for them, just about the time they got the hang of it, they were redundant. But wise grandparents know that in truth their role has changed: they have moved from being the coach at the side of the track to shouting encouragement from the grandstand. And while listening to advice graciously given, we have to have confidence in our own parenting – our children are our responsibility.

Then there's the problem of 'too far away' – although it's harder, grandparenting at a distance needn't be as daunting as it may seem at first.

In fact technology makes grandparenting at a distance easier than ever, and those who are separated across the miles sometimes have as much interaction as those who live nearby. Particularly during the pandemic, many grandparents have of necessity become tech wizards overnight, staying in touch via Zoom. A family whose grandchildren live in different time zones have learnt how to use an iPad and now Facetime their grandchildren at a mutually convenient time every week. Another granny we know has created a story with her grandson. She would write a paragraph and email it to him, then he would write the next bit and so on. Yet another grandparent reminded me that even (perhaps especially) in this technological age, children love to receive letters. A real piece of paper, with real writing and your very own name on the envelope is enough to make any child feel special.

There are numerous ways of staying in touch but my favourite is a little idea devised by a grandmother for her small granddaughter:

> She made a brightly coloured wrap that had an outline of her own hands at either end. She told her granddaughter that at any time she could ask her mum to curl it around her and she would feel her nan's arms hugging her. She had no idea how important the present would become to a very insistent two-year-old. Every night, just as her grandmother who lives in Scotland is waking up, a small child in Sydney, Australia falls off to sleep with her nan's 'arms' wrapped tightly around her.[29]

It is true that grandparents can be a wonderful influence on our children, but it's not all one way. Ruth Goode put it beautifully: 'Our grandchildren accept us for ourselves, without rebuke or effort to change us, as no one in our entire lives has ever done, not our parents, siblings, spouses, friends – and hardly ever our own grown children.'

But it was Sam Levenson who managed to identify the reason for the magic that is so often found in this relationship: 'The reason grandparents and grandkids get along so well is because they have a common enemy.'

I think there's some truth in that!

29 Rob Parsons, *The Sixty Minute Grandparent*, Hodder, 2013, p86.

BE THE FIRST TO SAY SORRY

An Oscar for the worst line ever must surely go to the 1970s novel and film *Love Story* for the phrase: 'Love means never having to say you're sorry.' In fact, for all relationships, including that of parent and child, the reverse is true. Loving our children means often having to say we are sorry. Being able to recognize when we are in the wrong and to apologize for it is one of the most important lessons that we can hand on to our children.

When my children were small, I can remember many occasions when I sent them to the 'naughty step' (now also known as the 'thinking step') and told them to consider the error of their ways. After a suitable time of self-examination and reflection – one minute for each year of their age – they would need to apologize to the person they had wronged. But I also remember times when the boot was on the other foot and Richard or I overstepped the line and needed to apologize to them.

On one occasion, while one of our children was doing time on the step, I remember thinking that my reaction had been far from perfect, and I would do well to sit on the naughty step myself and consider my behaviour! At bedtime that night, I said sorry to the child in question and asked for their forgiveness. In later years they have told me how powerful that lesson was for them.

Whether we are the child or the parent we will make mistakes, and, intentionally or not, we will hurt others. The old proverb says 'love prospers when a fault is forgiven.'[30] If we, as their parents, demonstrate that we are quick to admit when we are in the wrong, we will enable our children to build healthy relationships themselves in years to come. So lead the way – be the first to say sorry.

30 Proverbs 17:9, NLT.

TAKE A WALK IN HIS MOCCASINS

The proverb 'Don't judge anyone until you have walked two moons in his moccasins', is allegedly Native American in origin, although we see different iterations of it in many cultures. It neatly describes the quality of empathy – the ability to see a situation through someone else's eyes, to be understanding of their feelings and their needs. As parents it is good to try to encourage empathy in our children.[31]

I discovered quickly that from the very beginning it can be hard work trying to teach our children to share and to think of others. Any thoughts of sitting back and enjoying a catch-up and coffee with another parent while the boys played happily together, sharing the contents of the box of cars, bricks or tub of Lego, generally remained a dream. There was a season of life when two of our children seemed to spend most of their time arguing about anything and everything. If my back was turned for a second there would be a bloodcurdling scream of, 'It's not faaaair! He – or she – hit me/bit me/kicked me.' I frequently wondered where we had gone wrong to have children who

---

31 R. Weissbourd and S. Jones, 'How Parents Can Cultivate Empathy in Children', *Harvard Graduate School of Education*, harvard.edu.

seemed unable to play nicely together. My skills as a referee became honed to rival those of the refs in the Premier League: yellow card warnings and the occasional red card send-off were used to try to resolve disputes and to keep the peace.

If you are at a stage in parenting when an uninterrupted coffee is nothing more than a distant dream, stick with it. This important quality of empathy comes from the relationship we have with our children during these formative years when we are trying to encourage them to see things from another's perspective.

I have a friend who has five children and has somehow engendered this generous spirit into her children from a young age. She tells me there is no magic formula, but that she has consistently and continually tried to model this attitude in her own life, and then also encouraged her children to do the same. She has asked them questions like: 'How do you think Katy feels not getting the part in the play?' or, 'Do you think what's going on for Jack at home means he's not very happy? Maybe that's why he was unkind today?' or, slightly further afield, 'Can you imagine how cold it must be for Ian selling *The Big Issue* in the snow?' While she may of course be blessed with compliant children, there is no doubt that her attitude has paid off. Like any family, they have their moments, but overall they are some of the most kind and thoughtful children that I know.

As our children get older, we can spot opportunities to help them develop this quality. We can talk to them about difficult friendships in the playground, issues of sibling rivalry, or help them imagine the situations of those less fortunate than themselves, helping them to see things from another's point of view.

As parents, the task of reinforcing good behaviour can sometimes feel relentless, so in those rare moments when we get a glimpse of the fruit of our efforts, it is even more rewarding. I have shared a number of our family's mistakes; allow me now to share an encouragement. It was a freezing day in January when we went to visit family in Birmingham. On the way home we stopped for a pizza. The waitress came and took our order, but there was a mix-up, and to his delight, one of our children ended up with not one but two giant pizzas. Not even he could eat both, and so we arranged to take it away in a box, planning to eat it in the car on the way home. We put on coats and had just left the restaurant when my son stopped in his tracks and ran across the road. I saw him give the pizza to a homeless person who was sheltering from the cold in a doorway. It was such a kind and generous gesture – and, at that particular moment in our parenting journey, such an encouragement for us to see that quality of empathy emerging in this child's life. At that moment I was proud of him … and I think heaven smiled as well.

SLOW DOWN,

YOU MOVE

TOO

FAST

Slow down, you move too fast

Many of us as parents can look back to 'lightbulb' moments: times when we see life in a different way, and which cause us to draw a line in the sand and resolve to live differently. Such a moment occurred for us when our children were five, seven, nine and eleven. Keen for them to be proficient in the water, I had made enquiries about swimming lessons. Other parents at school had recommended an excellent teacher, Kim, who ran classes on a Monday after school. The only drawback was that it was at a school pool on the far side of the city. Even more inconvenient was the fact that, because of their range of age and ability, the lessons for our four children would have to be separate – one after the other. This meant that every Monday we had to dash straight from school through rush-hour traffic, in order to set up camp in the hot, steamy, chlorine-filled atmosphere of the pool for several hours.

I would pass the time by taking a packed tea and getting the younger children to do their reading while the older children swam, but it did not make for the most restful start to the week. However, I was determined they should learn to swim and this seemed to be the only way to make it happen. Head down and blinkered, I persevered.

Before long the children were asking to do other after-school activities that 'everyone else' was doing: Brownies, Beavers, Cubs, judo, recorder, football, tennis, netball, drama and – the straw that broke the camel's back – gymnastics. Each of the activities required a trip in the car to deliver and collect the child/children and extra friends, and soon every day of the week was taken up with some activity. Without us making a conscious decision, we had drifted into living at an unsustainable pace.

There was no time just to 'be'. The lightbulb moment came when at a summer conference I heard a talk on the subject of 'Rhythms of life'. The speaker talked about the tyranny of busyness and the frantic pace of life that we lead, which not only takes its toll on us, but sucks everyone around us into our spinning vortex. As he spoke, my mind reflected on the Monday swimming marathon and other after-school activities that came a close second, and I resolved to make some changes to our family life.

We are fortunate to live near the centre of our community, and on our return I made the decision to limit after school activities to those we could walk to. Any activity that involved loading four children in the car and driving across the city, pressing through rush-hour traffic and then going through the entire procedure in reverse, would stop.

This simple decision didn't give me 'mother of the year award'. But it changed our lives. We found a swimming teacher at the local school, and although she may not have been as experienced or qualified as the excellent Kim, she did the job we wanted. While our children will never be in the Olympic swimming squad, they do all have badges on their towels as proof that they learnt to stay afloat, and we achieved it without imploding in the process.

Different families will have different pressures on their time and energies. There may be some things that are important and that we definitely want our children to do, and others that we are not so concerned about. The important thing is to find a rhythm that works for you in your particular season of family life. If you live apart from your child's other parent and the child's time is divided between two homes, it will be even more important to monitor their pace. Those parenting alone will generally be the sole decision-maker and provider of the resources to make any activities happen, and they may need to be even more ruthless in choosing what they can and cannot do. They may also need to be prepared to ask for help and support where necessary.

An unsustainable pace of life can creep up on us unawares. Take a stock check and ask yourself if you can keep going with your current routine. And then if necessary, take drastic action to change things. Your children may not be at every club and activity, but you and they will have time to breathe and just to be.

IT
TAKES
A
VILLAGE

It takes a village

I don't believe there ever was a 'golden age' of the family, but I do believe that bringing up children was easier when families lived near each other and they could rely on the wisdom and support of the extended family. Geographical distance, family breakdown, multiple caring responsibilities, and the long-hours culture have all contributed to there being less connectedness between families. Isolation and loneliness are increasingly the hallmarks of our society – not just for the elderly, but for many younger people as well, something that was made even more acute during lockdown. Half a century ago, if a young mother had a baby who wouldn't sleep, if a newly-married couple had the row of a century, or a child needed advice with a school project, there would most likely have been a grandparent, an uncle, an aunt or a cousin just down the road who would be able to give much-needed reassurance, advice and support. But today many are parenting without family or even friends nearby, and we are the poorer for it.

Despite being able to communicate across the world at the touch of a screen, parenting can feel a lonely business. One parent put it like this;

'I've got good friends but I don't feel I can ask them about problems I am facing with the kids. It's never earth-shattering stuff, and it's not that there's not loads of information out there; it's just having someone to talk to – somebody to say, "This is not just you – you're doing a great job."'

There is a lovely proverb: 'It takes a village to raise a child,' which has many variations in different African cultures. It recognizes that parenting is a shared responsibility – a communal affair – not just the concern of parents or grandparents, but of the extended family. Uncles, aunts, cousins, neighbours and friends can all be involved and all have a part to play. In the West we have much to learn from other cultures when it comes to parenting. Even if we do not have extended family of our own on our doorstep, we can be 'family' to others in our community, giving and receiving mutual help and support. Especially when the children are small, get all the help you can!

When each of our children were small, I sought out friends with children of a similar age, and arranged to spend time together. An unintended consequence was that our children benefitted from being part of another family and seeing how things were done differently. When the children were little, a

local parent and toddler group was a lifeline – especially when a few of us decided we'd had enough of the 'Mine's already walking/talking/doing calculus' routine. We started being honest with each other. What a relief to discover that tantrums, whining and foot-stamping were normal – and that was just the mothers! We also made friends with those who had children just a little older than ours. They were able to give us the benefit of their experience through some of the ordinary (and also extraordinary) moments of family life. They could offer remedies for unexplained rashes and allergies; tips for dealing with a child who wouldn't eat anything green, what to do when a child swallowed a button! Not to mention advice about which school to apply for and how to appeal when you don't get your first choice … and so on.

'It takes a village to raise a child.' Different people have joined our 'village' throughout our journey as parents, and no doubt there will be more to come – extended family, friends, grandparents, godparents, single people, married people, and students. Our lives – and the lives of our children – and we hope their lives too – have been the richer for it.

The truth of all this is beautifully expressed by a saying attributed to the Sukuma tribe from Tanzania: 'One knee does not bring up a child.'

Find those other knees!

PARENT WITH ELASTIC

Parent with elastic

Looking back, many of us will remember specific moments when our children took a significant step to independence. The feelings we had the first time we left them with a babysitter, the first sleepover, the first day at school or the first trip to town may be etched on our minds. We know that our task as parents is to encourage our children to move from dependence to independence, but it can be so hard!

As parents, we're hardwired to protect our children. It's as if we want to keep them on the end of a tight piece of string to make sure they stay safe and are equipped for every eventuality. But a wise friend once said to me, 'Don't use string, use elastic.' If we use string, then as they seek their independence, that string will go taut and eventually snap. But if we use elastic, it will gradually stretch as we give them more responsibility as they grow up.

I like the idea of parenting with elastic. It makes the road to independence much easier for our children and also for us. From the day they take those first few faltering steps, we are beginning a process that will ultimately end with them standing on their own two feet long-term.

We can start this process when they are quite young by giving them choices. For example, 'Do you want your drink in the blue cup or the yellow cup?' 'Would you like peas or beans for tea?' 'Do you want to take your bike or your scooter to the park?' You could also let them choose what to wear from a few options – even if the pink flowery, orange check, red spots and green striped combination will require sunglasses all round.

As they get older we can give them freedom to choose how to spend pocket money, what colour to paint their room, what music they listen to and how to spend their free time.

In giving our children choices appropriate to their age, we also give them the freedom to learn from the consequences of their decisions, which nudges them further along the road to independence. A friend who is a childminder teaches this to the children in her care: 'You can choose to put your wellies on now – good choice – and we can go out to the park. Or you can continue to lie on the floor – bad choice – and we will run out of time and not be able to go.' The key here is that if we give our children the choice, we need to be OK with either option – which is not always easy!

Our ultimate goal is to equip our children with the tools and the values they need to make good and wise choices in a world where choices are unlimited. Introducing them to the concept at an early age, will help them develop their decision-making muscles as the years go by. And it will help them (and us) be ready for the day when the choices they must make are far more significant.

There will undoubtedly be some mistakes made on the way, but for our children, learning lessons while we are around to pick up the pieces is generally easier than learning them once they have flown the nest and are away from our care. Parent with elastic – it's never too soon to start.

'Yeah, it's my mum and dad. They think I don't know they're following me...'

VALUES ARE
MORE OFTEN
CAUGHT
THAN
TAUGHT

Values are more often caught than taught

Visit any large company and in the lift or reception area you are likely to find a list of company values on display. Executives have often spent hours crafting this document, getting the wording exactly right to reflect the heart of their business. But a value statement is not worth the paper it is written on unless it is lived out by the people who work for the company. If I am kept waiting thirty minutes with no explanation, the statement in the lift that 'Our value is to give excellent service and to put the client first,' will sound a little hollow. A company's values need to be owned, lived and embodied by the representatives of the company themselves. The same is true of family values.

We were on the way to football and running late. The children had eaten the last loaf after school and there was now no bread for sandwiches for tomorrow. The high street was busy with nowhere to park, so I pulled in on a double yellow line and dashed into the supermarket. Two minutes later, wholemeal loaf (no bits) under my arm, I emerged to see a traffic warden peering in the car window. I gave him a profuse apology, which he graciously accepted with a warning not to repeat the escapade, and we headed off for the match. I thought nothing more of the incident until the evening, when one of our children questioned me in detail about why it had been OK for us to park on double yellow lines.

Their cross examination was worthy of a QC at the Old Bailey, and any futile attempts to justify my position were unconvincing. Guilty as charged. The child had been genuinely perplexed that I had 'broken the law', and I reflected later that evening the truth of the maxim that values are indeed more often 'caught than taught'. His young mind found it hard to distinguish between breaking a rule about parking on a yellow line and breaking a school rule about keeping off the grass or talking in assembly. I had to admit he had a point.

And the truth is that our children are watching. They notice if we contribute to the food bank on our supermarket shop or recycle our plastic. They notice if we point out if we have been undercharged when paying for something. They notice how we treat our friends, parents and colleagues.

I think of one family who had encouraged their children always to be generous. They had been collecting for a charitable appeal and had urged their offspring to sort through any clothes they had grown out of to donate to the cause. The following day their son came home from school wearing his trainers. He explained that he had put his brand-new school shoes in the Salvation Army collection bin. As she headed out to buy a new pair before the shops closed, I imagine those parents felt a mixture of exasperation and annoyance, but underpinning it all, a reassuring sense of pride that their family values were getting through.

There is a proverb which says, 'Train up a child in the way he should go: and when he is old he will not depart from it.'[32] Of course, it's not a guarantee, but the truth is that what we sow into our children's lives isn't wasted. We so often worry with our children that 'Nothing is going in!' but the problem can be the opposite: not a word is lost. What we say and do – especially

32 Proverbs 22:6 (ESV).

in these primary years – has a profound effect upon their lives, forever. William Wordsworth was right when he wrote 'The child is father of the man.'[33] So often what is poured into our lives when we are very young, especially by example, forms character and values that will last down the years.

As our children get older, they may not share our values, but we are their parents and it's important that they know what we believe. If faith is important to us, we will want to share it with them. We may want to teach them to pray, but more importantly let them catch us praying; let them see the reality of faith in our lives. We can pass on what we believe about the environment, about relationships, about money, or simply about the things that we believe are right and wrong.

If you haven't ever done so, it is worth taking a moment to think what your family values are. What are the things that you believe are important, the non-negotiables that you seek to live by?

A friend recently bought us a black and white picture, which now takes pride of place in our kitchen. It reads:

Have hope.
Be strong.
Play hard.
Live in the moment.
Smile often.
Dream big.
Remember you are loved.
And never, never give up.

33 William Wordsworth, 'My heart leaps up when I behold', *Poems, in Two Volumes*, Longman, Hurst, Rees and Orme, 1807.

If we had designed it ourselves we would no doubt have added some more, but these values are not a bad place to start in giving our family some bearings for life – compass readings that we can return to when the storms of life come our way. But in the same way as a company's values are worthless unless they are owned and embodied, our children will only absorb the family values that they see us living.

The values we live by will be caught rather than taught. We sometimes worry that our children aren't listening to us, but the sobering truth is that not a word or an action is lost.

'LOOK MUMMY, IT'S YOUR FRIEND WHO DOESN'T KNOW HOW TO DRESS.'

TAKE A
SECOND
LOOK

Take a second look

A young girl was sitting in a chemistry lesson at Edgbaston High School. The lesson had only just begun when her teacher burst through the door to break the news that she been awarded the Nobel Peace Prize. At seventeen she was the youngest person ever to have received this honour. Her name was Malala Yousafzai.

Malala was born in Pakistan, and from a young age she campaigned for the right for girls to have an education. She gained an increasing public platform and became well known for her views.

The 9th October 2012 had been another ordinary school day in the Swat Valley in Northwest Pakistan for Malala. She walked out of the school gates as usual and climbed onto a small bus for the short trip home. She squeezed up on the benches with her friends, and they chattered about the day and the exam they had just sat. As the bus passed a clearing, a man flagged it down. Another approached the back of the van, swung onto the tailboard, and leaned in. Brandishing a Colt .45, he shouted to the terrified schoolgirls, 'Who is Malala?'

No one said anything but several of the girls looked at Malala – she was the only one with her face not covered. The gunman shot her at point blank range. She was in a critical condition, her life hanging in the balance. She had paid a terrible price for her incredible stand for the right of girls to receive an education. She was flown to a hospital in Peshawar and then brought to Birmingham where she has made an astonishing recovery, and continued her fight for the rights of girls and women.

Where did her resilience and courage come from?

In her autobiography, Malala writes that for most Pashtuns it's a gloomy day when a daughter is born. The day Malala was born, the people in the village commiserated with her mother and nobody congratulated her father.[34]

But her father, Ziauddin, looked into her eyes, then took a longer, second look. He fell in love. This man recognized the potential in his daughter. He told people, 'I know there is something different about this child'. He decided the name that he would give her: Malala means 'heroic freedom fighter.' Then he did something incredible. That second look spurred him on to defy cultural norms. He asked friends to come round to celebrate her birth, and to throw coins into her crib – something that was usually only done for boys. Each coin was a statement of the love and confidence he had in her. Each coin said, 'You have gifts. You have an identity. You have a destiny to fulfil … You are special.'

The affirmation and significance represented by those coins began when she was in her crib but their effect on her has lasted all her life. It has shaped her and has allowed her to become the woman she is today. Secure in her identity, she has become known as an icon of courage and hope.

Malala's father gave a TED talk about his daughter. He was asked what he had done as a father to instil such resilience in her. He replied, 'Don't ask me what I did; ask me what I did not do. I did not clip her wings.'[35]

34 Malala Yousafzai and Christina Lamb, *I am Malala: The Girl Who Stood Up for Education and was Shot by the Taliban*, Terbitan Little, Brown and Company, 2013, p9.
35 Ziauddin Yousafzai, 'My Daughter Malala', *TED Talks*, 2014, ted.com.

He may have not clipped her wings, but of course so much of what Malala became was because of the things he did. He refused to passively accept what his culture said to him about his daughter's future, and he dared to believe differently. He dared to take a second look. The coins in the crib, the belief that he had in her, gave Malala the message: 'You have value, you can stand tall, you are special.'

What an incredible gift to send a child into the world with. Spot your child's potential. They may not fit into society's definition of success. They may not be great sportsmen or women, they may not be gifted academically, or look the part. They may struggle with difficulties that make life a challenge – but each child is unique and has gifts to offer the world.

Always take a second look.

SNOW
LEOPARD
MOMENTS

Snow leopard moments

I saw a film recently that has a lovely scene in it. A photographer for a popular magazine desperately wants a picture of a snow leopard. Snow leopards are beautiful animals that live in the mountains of Central and South Asia. They have green eyes and thick, smoky grey fur with dark grey spots, and they are an endangered species.

The photographer's ambition is to take a picture of this animal. He makes a journey into the mountains, settles down in his tent and waits and waits. A friend has been looking for him and comes and joins him. Days and days go by and there is no sign of this animal. Then, one evening, in a breathtaking moment, the snow leopard appears. Its magnificent form fills the lens of the camera. The friends hold their breath and watch.

The snow leopard looks full on at the camera, lingers for thirty seconds, and then disappears back to where he came from. The spell is broken as the friend turns to him astounded and says, 'You didn't take the picture!' The photographer replies, 'It was such an incredible moment, I couldn't do it. I just needed to enjoy the moment.'

We enjoyed that film while on a family holiday in a seaside cottage in Wales. While we were there, we had the use of a couple of sea kayaks and most afternoons we would paddle out through the waves to try to catch some fish. We experimented with different weights, different lines and different bait, but all in vain. By the end of the week, all we had caught was a solitary miniature mackerel. On the final evening, the sun was setting, the sea was calm and the weather glorious (who needs the Med?), and we decided to give the kayaks one last outing. We had been paddling for about ten minutes when suddenly a fish jumped up just ahead of us, its silver scales catching the light of the setting sun. It was followed by another and then another and another, and before we knew it, we were surrounded by hundreds and hundreds of jumping bass. The sea was teeming. We reached for the lines, but as we did so we felt a check in our spirits. Richard turned to me and said, 'This is a "snow leopard moment". Let's just enjoy it.'

In our children's lives there are so many snow leopard moments. I can understand that we may want to record their first steps, their starring role in the nativity play, or their efforts in the final of the egg and spoon race on Sports Day, but sometimes the real place for those things is in our hearts and not on the camera. Have your own 'internal camera' and take time to capture those special times that are often found in the everyday moments of family life. Perhaps it's our little girl tucking her doll in at night; the chocolate-smeared grin of our six-year-old as he polishes off the leftover cupcake icing; or the sight of our children peacefully asleep without a care in the world.

These snow leopard moments are precious. Watch out for them, and feel and enjoy them to the full. Try not to miss a single one.

163

Give them roots

On any journey, we need to start with the end in mind. And as parents, when life is all-consuming, it's good sometimes to pause, step back, and remind ourselves that what we are doing now is equipping our children to be secure, confident adults who can go on to fulfil their potential and to build strong relationships in years to come.

A friend once sent me a lovely quote that I have found so helpful over the years. It said this:

'There are two things we should give our children. One is roots and the other wings.'

In these formative years, our focus as parents is to help them put down strong roots that will give them security and strength in the future. We do this by building their character and placing values in their lives. Character and values aren't built overnight. There's a lesson we can learn from the bamboo tree. After the seed for this extraordinary tree is planted in the ground, you see nothing for four years, except for a tiny shoot coming out from the bulb. During those four years, all the energy and growth goes into a huge root system that grows deep and wide under the earth. But then, in the fifth year, the tree grows to eighty feet tall.

As we invest in our children's lives in these primary years, we may not see the results straight away. We may feel exasperated at our children's behaviour and it can feel like we are banging our heads against a brick wall. But we can trust that much of the work is being done in secret, underground. Strong roots are growing in their lives that in time will anchor them securely when they navigate what can be the stormy weather of the teenage years and beyond.

'That's not quite what I meant, sweetheart...'

CARPE DIEM

One of the roles for which Hollywood actor Robin Williams will be best remembered is the maverick English teacher, John Keating, in the film *Dead Poets Society*. There's an inspiring scene when he leads the boys out of the classroom and into a corridor lined with row upon row of framed photographs of boys that have gone before. He gathers the class together, looks at the photos and says:

> They're not that different from you, are they? Same haircuts. Full of hormones, just like you. Invincible, just like you feel. The world is their oyster. They believe they're destined for great things, just like many of you. Their eyes are full of hope, just like you. Did they wait until it was too late to make from their lives even one iota of what they were capable? Because, you see, gentlemen, these boys are now fertilizing daffodils. But if you listen real close, you can hear them whisper their legacy to you. Go on, lean in. Listen, you hear it? … Carpe … hear it? Carpe … Carpe diem. Seize the day, boys.[36]

Without a shadow of doubt, if instead of a classroom of students John Keating had been speaking to a group of parents no doubt

36 *Dead Poets Society*, directed by Peter Weir, Buena Vista Pictures Distribution, 1989.

he would have whispered the same message – perhaps with even more urgency: *Carpe diem*. Seize the day.

When Richard and I started out as parents, older and wiser friends would say to me, 'Don't wish the time away; it goes so fast.' And as we have journeyed through the ups and downs of family life – the sleepless nights, the toddler tantrums, the first day at school, the rollercoaster of the teenage years – I confess there have been many times when I have wanted to do just that and fast-forward to a slower day. But with the passage of time I now see things a little differently and understand the wisdom of that advice.

Some time ago, a parent said to me, 'I hear people talk about the empty nest. At the moment I've got a baby that won't stop crying, a two-year-old that is determined to feed Weetabix to her hamster and a teenager that seems to have lost the ability to speak. That empty nest sounds pretty attractive!' I sympathize. And yet even as she spoke, my mind went to something I'd heard another mother say some years ago:

'Remember that bedroom strewn with crisp packets, scrunched up homework, muddy sports kit, damp towels, odd socks (and shoes!) and enough dirty underwear to start an epidemic? Of course you do. You have yelled for it to be tidied, bribed for it to be tidied and prayed for it to be tidied. Well one day it will be – too tidy!

You'll be free! No more birthday cakes to make in the shape of cartoon characters, nativity costumes to conjure up using old curtains and a tea towel and no more solemn goldfish burials in the garden. You'll have time to yourself: no buggies to manoeuvre into overcrowded shops, no haircuts with a wriggling toddler on your knee, no four-year-olds wandering half asleep into your bedroom, no leaving a drink for Father

Christmas, no knotted hair after swimming, no trying to skip pages reading a bedtime story and getting found out.

Honey sandwiches, hide and seek, stories under the sheets, tonsils, school runs, shoelaces, lunch boxes, croup, milk teeth, cut knees, first periods and maths periods – all gone. Bringing up young children will be all done and dusted.

One day you'll say "It's time you kids grew up!"

And they will.'

The years of childhood go by so quickly. Don't wish the time away; be kind to yourself, lay down regrets. Tonight, even, if you are so tired you can barely keep your eyes open a moment longer, just pause. Take a moment to look back over today. Find something, however small, to celebrate, to enjoy. And look ahead to tomorrow and resolve to do the same. Make the most of every moment that you can. *v*.

And take heart – nobody knows your child like you, and nobody loves them like you. Have confidence in your parenting. There is no one way to be a perfect parent – but there are a hundred ways to be a great parent. There is no task more important than bringing up the next generation. Enjoy!

'seeing as the kids are at your parents, I'm going to seize the day and stay in bed for all of it!'

Muddy
Pearl

Care for the Family is a national charity which aims to promote strong family life and help those who face family difficulties. Working throughout the UK and the Isle of Man, we provide parenting, relationship and bereavement support through our events, courses, training and other resources. For more information, and to explore our wide range of resources on all aspects of family life, visit our website at **www.careforthefamily.org.uk.**

Also from Katharine Hill:

If You Forget Everything Else Remember This:
Building a Great Marriage

BY KATHARINE HILL

192 PAGES | £9.99 | ISBN 978-1-910012-54-3

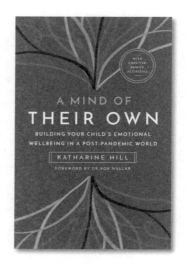

A Mind of Their Own

BY KATHARINE HILL

192 PAGES | £12.99 | ISBN 978-1-910012-31-4

ALSO AVAILABLE AS AN EBOOK

Left to Their Own Devices

BY KATHARINE HILL

208 PAGES | £12.99 | ISBN 978-1-914553-06-6

ALSO AVAILABLE AS AN EBOOK

The Really Really Busy Person's Book On Parenting
BY KATHARINE HILL AND ROB PARSONS]
144 PAGES | £7.50 | ISBN 978-1-910012-28-4

The Really Really Busy Person's Book On Marriage
BY KATHARINE HILL AND ROB PARSONS
144 PAGES | £7.50 | ISBN 978-1-910012-28-4

The Little Book for Really Really Brilliant Grandparents
BY KATHARINE HILL AND ROB PARSONS
144 PAGES | £9.99 | ISBN 978-1-910012-28-4